WHAT IS
REFORMED
THEOLOGY?

Among Other Books by the Author

WHAT IS

REFORMED

THEOLOGY?

UNDERSTANDING THE BASICS

R. C. SPROUL

BakerBooks

a division of Baker Publishing Group
Grand Rapids, Michigan

Published by Baker Books
a division of Baker Publishing Group
P.O. Box 6287, Grand Rapids, MI 49516-6287
www.bakerbooks.com

Repackaged edition published 2016

Printed in the United States of America

Library of Congress Cataloging-in-Publication Data
Names: Sproul, R. C. (Robert Charles), 1939– author.
Title: What is reformed theology? : understanding the basics / R.C. Sproul.
Other titles: Grace unknown
Description: Repackaged [edition]. | Grand Rapids : Baker Books, 2016. | Originally
    published as: Grace unknown. Grand Rapids, Mich. : Baker Books, c1997. |
    Includes bibliographical references and index.
Identifiers: LCCN 2016014488 | ISBN 9780801018466 (pbk.)
Subjects: LCSH: Theology, Doctrinal—Popular works. | Reformed
    Church—Doctrines.
Classification: LCC BT77 .S7184 2016 | DDC 230/.42—dc23
LC record available at https://lccn.loc.gov/2016014488

Scripture quotations are from the New King James Version®. Copyright © 1982 by Thomas Nelson, Inc. Used by permission. All rights reserved.

The proprietor is represented by the literary agency of Wolgemuth & Associates, Inc.

19   20   21   22   7   6   5   4

In memory of
James Montgomery Boice

Contents

Contents

ILLUSTRATIONS

Figures

Tables

INTRODUCTION

Reformed Theology Is *a Theology*

What is Reformed theology? The purpose of this book is to provide a simple answer to this question. *What Is Reformed Theology?* is not a textbook on systematic theology, nor a detailed, comprehensive exposition of each and every article of Reformation doctrine. It is, instead, a compendium, a shorthand introduction to the crystallized essence of Reformation theology.

In the nineteenth century theologians and historians, busy with a comparative analysis of world religions, sought to distill the essence of religion itself and reduce Christianity to its least common denominator. The term *Wesen* (being or essence) appeared in a plethora of German theological studies, including Adolf Harnack's book *What Is Christianity?* Harnack reduced Christianity to two essential affirmations, the universal fatherhood of God and

11

the universal brotherhood of man, neither of which is espoused by the Bible in the sense articulated by Harnack.[1]

A Theology, Not a Religion

This movement to reduce religion to its essence had a subtle but dramatic effect. The study of religion supplanted the study of theology in the academic world. This change was subtle in that, to the general populace, religion and theology were the same thing, so people felt no dramatic impact. Even in the academic world the shift was widely accepted with barely a whimper.

Several years ago I was invited to address the faculty of a prominent midwestern college with a rich Christian and Reformed tradition. The school was without a president, and the faculty was engaged in a self-study to define the college's identity. They asked me to address the question, "What are the distinctives of a uniquely 'Christian' education?"

Before my lecture the dean showed me around the campus. When we entered the faculty office building, I noticed one office with these words stenciled on the door: Department of Religion.

That evening as I spoke to the faculty I said: "During my tour of your facility I noticed an office door that announced 'Department of Religion.' My question is twofold. First, was that department always called the Department of Religion?"

My inquiry was greeted by silence and blank stares. At first I thought no one was able to answer my question. Finally an elder statesman of the faculty raised his hand

and said, "No, it used to be called the 'Department of Theology.' We changed it about thirty years ago."

"Why did you change it?" I asked.

No one in the room had any idea, nor did they seem to care. The tacit assumption was, "It doesn't really matter."

I reminded the faculty that there is a profound difference between the study of theology and the study of religion. Historically the study of religion has been subsumed under the headings of anthropology, sociology, or even psychology. The academic investigation of religion has sought to be grounded in a scientific-empirical method. The reason for this is quite simple. Human activity is part of the phenomenal world. It is activity that is visible, subject to empirical analysis. Psychology may not be as concrete as biology, but human behavior in response to beliefs, urges, opinions, and so forth can be studied in accordance with the scientific method.

To state it more simply, the study of religion is chiefly the study of a certain kind of *human behavior*, be it under the rubric of anthropology, sociology, or psychology. The study of theology, on the other hand, is the study of God. Religion is anthropocentric; theology is theocentric. The difference between religion and theology is ultimately the difference between God and man—hardly a small difference.

Again, it is a difference of subject matter. The subject matter of theology proper is *God*; the subject matter of religion is *man*.

A major objection to this simplification may arise immediately: Doesn't the study of theology involve the study of what human beings say about God?

The Study of Scripture

We answer this question with one word: "Partially." We study theology in several ways. The first is by studying the Bible. Historically the Bible was received by the church as a normative depository of divine revelation. Its ultimate Author was thought to be God himself. This is why the Bible was called the *verbum Dei* (Word of God) or the *vox Dei* (voice of God). It was considered to be a product of divine self-disclosure. The information contained within it comes, not as a result of human empirical investigation or human speculation, but by supernatural *revelation*. It is called revelation because it comes from the mind of God to us.

Historically Christianity claimed to be and was received as *revealed truth*, not truth discovered via human insight or ingenuity. Paul begins his Epistle to the Romans with these words: "Paul, a servant of Jesus Christ, called to be an apostle, separated to the gospel of God . . ." (Rom. 1:1). What does the phrase "gospel *of* God" mean? Does the word *of* indicate possession or does it mean simply "about"? Is Paul saying that the gospel is something *about* God or something *from* God? Historic Christianity would consider this question an exercise in the fallacy of the false dilemma or the either/or fallacy. Classical Christianity would say that the gospel is a message that is both *about* God and *from* God.

At the same time the church has always recognized that the Bible was not written by the finger of God. God did not write a book, have it published by the Celestial Publishing Company, and then drop it to earth by parachute. The church has always acknowledged that the Scriptures were composed and written by human authors.

The burning issue today is this: Were these human authors writing their own unaided opinions and insights, or were they uniquely endowed as agents of revelation, writing under the inspiration and superintendence of God? If we say that the Bible is a product of only human opinion and insight, we can still speak about biblical theology in the sense that the Bible contains human teaching about God, but we can no longer speak about biblical revelation. If God is the ultimate Author of the Bible, we can speak of *both* biblical revelation *and* biblical theology. If man is the ultimate author, then we are restricted to speaking about biblical theology or *theologies*. If that is the case, we could justly regard biblical theology as a subdivision of religion, as one aspect of human studies about God.

The Study of History

A second way we study theology is historically. Historical theology does involve a study of what people who are not inspired agents of revelation teach about God. We examine historical councils, creeds, and writings of theologians such as Augustine, Thomas Aquinas, Martin Luther, John Calvin, Karl Barth, and others. We study various theological traditions to learn how each one understood the content of biblical theology. On the one hand this may be called a study of religion in the sense that it is the study of religious *thought*.

We may be motivated to study historical theology merely to understand the history of religious thinking. In this scenario the subject matter is human opinion. Or we may be motivated to study historical theology to learn what others have learned about God. In this scenario the subject matter is God and the things of God.

Of course we could be motivated to study historical theology by a combination of these two or for other reasons. The point is that we can have either a theological interest primarily, or a religious interest, as long as we recognize that they are not identical.

The Study of Nature

A third way of studying theology is by studying nature for clues it gives about God's character. This we call *natural theology*. Natural theology refers to information about God that is gleaned from nature. People approach natural theology from two distinct vantage points. First there are those who view natural theology as a theology derived from sheer human speculation—by unaided reason reflecting philosophically on nature. Second are those who, in accord with the historic approach to natural theology, see it as the product of and based on natural revelation. Revelation is something God does. It is his action of self-disclosure.

Natural theology is something *we* acquire. It is the result of either human speculation, viewing nature as a neutral object-in-itself, or of human reception of information given by the Creator in and through his creation. The second approach views nature not as a neutral object-in-itself that is mute, but as a theater of divine revelation where information is transmitted through the created order.

From the sixteenth century until the beginning of the twentieth, no Reformed theologian I know of denied the validity of natural theology derived from natural revelation.

The strong antipathy in our day to theology based on un-aided human speculation has brought in its wake a wide-spread and wholesale rejection of *all* natural theology.

This departure, in part a reaction against Enlighten-ment rationalism, is a departure from historic Reformed theology and from biblical theology.

Both Roman Catholicism and historic Reformed theology embraced natural theology gleaned from natu-ral revelation. The reason for this substantial agreement is because the Bible, which both sides regarded as a special revelation, clearly teaches that, in addition to God's reve-lation of himself in Scripture, there is also the sphere of divine revelation found in nature.

Classical theology made an acute distinction between *special revelation* and *general revelation*. The two kinds of revelation are distinguished by the terms *special* and *general* because of the difference in content-scope and in the audience of each.

Special revelation is special because it provides spe-cific information about God that cannot be found in na-ture. Nature does not teach us God's plan for salvation; Scripture does. We learn many more specifics about the character and activity of God from Scripture than we can ever glean from creation. The Bible is also called special revelation because the information contained in it is un-known by people who have never read the Bible or had it proclaimed to them.

General revelation is general because it reveals general truths about God and because its audience is universal. Every person is exposed to some degree to God's reve-lation in creation.

The most germane biblical basis for a general or natural revelation is Paul's statement in Romans:

> For the wrath of God is revealed from heaven against all ungodliness and unrighteousness of men, who suppress the truth in unrighteousness, because what may be known of God is manifest in them, for God has shown it to them. For since the creation of the world His invisible attributes are clearly seen, being understood by the things that are made, even His eternal power and Godhead, so that they are without excuse, because, although they knew God, they did not glorify Him as God. (Rom. 1:18–21)

God directs his wrath to mankind because of their repression of natural revelation. God may be known because he has "shown" what may be known about himself. This showing or revealing is "manifest" or clear. In creation God's invisible attributes, though invisible, are "clearly seen"—that is, they are seen by or through the things that God made. This is almost universally understood to mean that God clearly reveals himself in and through nature, that there is a general or natural revelation.

Does this manifest revelation "get through" to us and yield any knowledge of God? Paul does not leave us in doubt. He says this divine revelation is "seen" and "understood." To see and understand something is to have some kind of knowledge about it.

Paul says that "they *knew* God," making it plain that natural revelation yields a natural theology or a natural knowledge of God. God's wrath is present, not because men fail to receive his natural revelation, but because, after receiving this knowledge, mankind fails to act appropriately. They refuse to honor God or be grateful to him. They suppress the truth of God, and as Paul later says, "They did not like to retain God in their knowledge" (Rom. 1:28).

People reject the natural knowledge they have of God. This rejection, however, does not annihilate either the revelation or the knowledge itself. The sin of mankind is in refusing to *acknowledge* the *knowledge* they have. They act against the truth that God reveals and they clearly receive.

The believer who acquiesces in special revelation is now in a posture to respond properly to general revelation. In this regard the Christian should be the most diligent student of both special and natural revelation. Our theology should be informed by both the Bible and nature. The two come from the same revelatory source, God himself. The two revelations do not conflict; they reflect the harmony of God's self-disclosures.

A final way we study theology is through speculative philosophical theology. This approach can be driven either by a prior commitment to natural revelation or by a conscious attempt to counter natural revelation. The first is a legitimate reason for the Christian; the second is an act of treason against God, based on the pretense of human autonomy.

In all these various approaches there can be a study of theology rather than a mere analysis of religion. When we engage in the quest to understand God, it is theology. When our quest is limited to understanding how people react to theology, it is religion.

Queen of the Sciences

The study of theology *includes* a study of mankind, but this is from a theological perspective. We could order our science as in figure 0.1. There are many subdivisions of the discipline of theology, one of which is anthropology. The modern approach looks more like figure 0.2, in which theology is a subset of anthropology. These two paradigms illustrate the difference between a theocentric view of man and an anthropocentric view of religion and God.

Fig. 0.1

God-Centered View of Theology

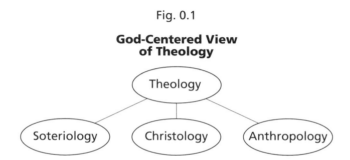

In the classical curriculum theology is the queen of the sciences and all other disciplines are her handmaidens. In the modern curriculum man is king and the former queen is relegated to a peripheral status of insignificance.

In his monumental work *No Place for Truth*, David F. Wells writes,

> The disappearance of theology from the life of the Church, and the orchestration of that disappearance by some of its leaders, is hard to miss today but, oddly enough, not easy to prove. It is hard to miss in the evangelical world—in the vacuous worship that is so prevalent, for example, in the shift from God to the self as the central focus of faith,

in the psychologized preaching that follows this shift, in the erosion of its conviction, in its strident pragmatism, in its inability to think incisively about the culture, in its reveling in the irrational.[2]

Fig. 0.2

**Man-Centered View
of Theology**

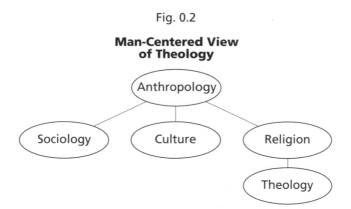

Citing Ian T. Ramsey, Wells speaks of our present condition as a church without theology and a theology without God.[3]

A church without theology or a theology without God are simply not options for the Christian faith. One can have religion without God or theology, but one cannot have Christianity without them.

Theology and Religion at Sinai

To further illustrate the difference between theology and religion, let us examine briefly a famous incident in the history of Israel. In Exodus 24 we read: "Then Moses went up into the mountain, and a cloud covered the mountain. Now the glory of the LORD rested on Mount Sinai, and the cloud covered it six days. And on the seventh day He called to Moses out of the midst of the cloud. The sight of the glory of the LORD was like a consuming fire on the top of the mountain in the eyes of the children of Israel. So Moses went into the midst of the cloud and went up into the mountain. And Moses was on the mountain forty days and forty nights" (Exod. 24:15–18).

In this episode Moses ascends the same mountain he formerly visited amid smoke, thunder, and lightning. He was summoned to a meeting with God. The glory of God was manifest to the people as a consuming fire. But God himself was hidden from them, concealed by clouds.

Moses entered the cloud cover. His mission was one of pure theology. He was pursuing God himself. In light of this display, we must assume that the people left behind were not atheists. Aware of God's reality and his saving work, they were neither secularists nor liberals. They were the evangelicals of the day, recipients of special revelation and participants in the redemptive exodus.

Later in this narrative, however, we read of a startling shift in their behavior: "Now when the people saw that Moses delayed coming down from the mountain, the people gathered together to Aaron, and said to him, 'Come, make us gods that shall go before us; for as for this Moses, the man who brought us up out of the land of Egypt, we do not know what has become of him'" (Exod. 32:1).

What follows is an unprecedented act of apostasy: the making and worshiping of a golden calf. This was an exercise in religion, one that focused its worship on a creature. When they made their priceless, state-of-the-art calf, they said, "This is your god, O Israel, that brought you out of the land of Egypt!" (Exod. 32:4).

Notice that this is a theological affirmation. They claimed that the golden calf was God and that the calf had delivered them from bondage. This theology was blatantly false. It was also evidence that false religion flows out of false theology. Their calf was an idolatrous graven image, which exchanged the truth of God for a lie and traded the glory of God for the glory of an artistic creation.

There is much wrong here. In the first place, the bull was the sacred image of the heathen gods of Egypt. By making their own bull-idol, Israel conformed their religion to the world around them. Their new religion was now relevant. They had a god that they could control. They made it and they could discard or destroy it. The cow gave no law and demanded no obedience. It had no wrath or justice or holiness to be feared. It was deaf, dumb, and impotent. But at least it could not intrude on their fun and call them to judgment. This was a religion designed by men, practiced by men, and ultimately useless for men. Theirs was a theology and a religion without God. It had the elements of religious practice, but what was worshiped was not God. The true God had been stripped of his real character by the people's vacuous theology.

A further irony is seen in the reason for Moses's delay in returning from the mountains—from chapter 24 until this moment in chapter 32, Moses was receiving detailed instructions from God. These instructions focused on one thing: true worship. God was giving detailed commandments concerning the tabernacle, the Aaronic priesthood, the liturgy of worship, and the sanctity of the Sabbath.

While Moses was learning sound theology, the first man consecrated as high priest, Aaron, was building an altar to a golden calf. God was instructing Moses in proper religion that is based on a theology of truth.

David F. Wells notes, "In the past, the doing of theology encompassed three essential aspects in both the Church and the academy: (1) a confessional element, (2) reflection on this confession, and (3) the cultivation of a set of virtues that are grounded in the first two elements."[4]

When we speak of Reformed theology, we will view it from this historical perspective. We begin our study by asserting that Reformed theology is first and foremost a *theology*. As a theology it has confessional, reflective, and behavioral aspects.

The rest of this book will examine why this theology is called Reformed, but not until we repeat once more that it is a theology, not merely a religion without theology. It is driven first and foremost by its understanding of the character of God.

PART 1

FOUNDATIONS OF REFORMED THEOLOGY

1

CENTERED ON GOD

Reformed theology is systematic. The science of systematic theology is so called because it attempts to understand doctrine in a coherent and unified manner. It is not the goal of systematic theology to impose on the Bible a system derived from a particular philosophy. Rather its goal is to discern the interrelatedness of the teachings of Scripture itself. Historically the systematic theologian assumed that the Bible is the Word of God, and as such is not filled with internal conflict and confusion. Though many themes are treated by many different human authors over a vast period of time, the message that emerges was thought to be from God and therefore coherent and consistent. In this case consistency is not considered to be the "hobgoblin of little minds." God's mind is by no means a little one.

In the modern church the assumptions of the past are not always retained. Many have rejected the divine inspiration of Scripture and with it any commitment to a unified revelation. When one approaches the Bible as purely a human document, one need not reconcile the teachings of its various authors. From this viewpoint, systematic theology usually is an attempt to explain the Bible in light of and under the control of a system brought to the Bible from the outside. Others eschew systems altogether and embrace a theology that is self-consciously relativistic and pluralistic. They set biblical authors in opposition to each other, and they see the Bible itself as a collection of conflicting theologies.

Table 1.1
The First Foundation Stone

1 **Centered on God**
2 Based on God's Word alone
3 Committed to faith alone
4 Devoted to Jesus Christ
5 Structured by three covenants

Classical Reformed theology, on the other hand, does regard the Bible as God's Word. Though it recognizes that the Scriptures were penned by different writers at different times, the divine inspiration of the whole carries with it the unity and coherency of the truth of God. Therefore the Reformed quest for a systematic theology is an effort to discover and define the system of doctrine taught internally by the Scriptures themselves.

Because theology is systematic, every doctrine of the faith touches in some way every other doctrine. For example, how we understand the person of Christ affects how we understand his work of redemption. If we view Jesus merely as a great human teacher, then we are inclined to see his mission as primarily one of moral instruction or influence. If we regard him as the Son of God incarnate, then this frames our understanding of his mission.

Conversely, our understanding of the work of Christ also influences our understanding of his person.

Perhaps no doctrine has greater bearing on all other doctrines than the doctrine of God. How we understand the nature and character of God himself influences how we understand the nature of man, who bears God's image; the nature of Christ, who works to satisfy the Father; the nature of salvation, which is effected by God; the nature of ethics, the norms of which are based on God's character; and a myriad of other theological considerations, all drawing on our understanding of God.

Reformed theology is first and foremost theocentric rather than anthropocentric. That is, it is God-centered rather than man-centered. This God-centeredness by no means denigrates the value of human beings. On the contrary it establishes their value. Reformed theology has often been characterized as having a low view of mankind due to its insistence on humanity's fallenness and radical corruption. I have argued that Reformed theology has the highest possible view of humanity. Because we have such a lofty view of God, we care so much about the one created in his image. Reformed theology takes sin seriously because it takes God seriously and because it takes people seriously. Sin offends God and violates human beings. Both of these are serious matters.

Reformed theology maintains a high view of the worth and dignity of human beings. It differs radically at this point from all forms of humanism in that humanism assigns an *intrinsic* dignity to man, while Reformed theology sees the dignity of man as being *extrinsic*. That is to say, man's dignity is not inherent. It does not exist in and of itself. Ours is a derived, dependent, and received dignity. In and of ourselves we are of the dust. But God has assigned a remarkable value and worth to us as his creatures made in his image. He is the source of our life and our very being. He has cloaked us with a robe of value and worth.

Sometimes a dispute arises concerning the goal or purpose of God's plan of redemption. The question is posed: Is the goal of redemption the manifestation of the glory of God? Or is it the manifestation of the value of fallen humanity? Is the goal man-centered or God-centered? If we were forced to choose between these options, we would have to opt for the primacy of God's glory. The good news is that we are not forced to choose. In God's plan of redemption, we see both his concern for the well-being of his creation and his concern for the manifestation of his own glory. God's glory is manifested in and through his work of redemption. It is even manifested in the punishment of the wicked. God displays with startling majesty both his ineffable grace and his righteous judgment. Even in God's judgment he vindicates the value of man by punishing the evil that so despoils human life.

Though I am not enamored with the use of paradox in theological discourse, I will not shrink from stating one now. Though there is not much in the Reformed doctrine of God that differs significantly from the doctrine confessed by other Christian communions, the most distinctive aspect of Reformed theology is its doctrine of God. How can this statement be true? Though the Reformed doctrine of God is not all that different from that of other confessional bodies, the way this doctrine functions in Reformed theology is unique. Reformed theology applies the doctrine of God relentlessly to all other doctrines, making it the chief control factor in all theology.

For example, I have never met a confessing Christian unwilling to affirm that God is sovereign. Sovereignty is a divine attribute confessed almost universally in historic Christianity. When we press the doctrine of divine sovereignty into other realms of theology, however, it is often weakened or destroyed altogether. I have often heard it said, "God's sovereignty is limited by human freedom." In this statement God's sovereignty is not absolute. It is bounded by a limit and that limit is human freedom.

Reformed theology indeed insists that a real measure of freedom has been assigned to man by the Creator. But that freedom is not absolute and man is not autonomous. Our freedom is always and everywhere limited by God's sovereignty. God is free and we are free. But God is more free than we are. When our freedom bumps up against God's sovereignty, our freedom must yield. To say that God's sovereignty is limited by man's freedom is to make man sovereign. To be sure, the statement that God's sovereignty is limited by human freedom may simply express the idea that God does not in fact violate human freedom. But of course this is a different matter. If God never violates human freedom, it is not because of any limit on his sovereignty. It is because he sovereignly decrees not to. He has the authority and power to do it if he wants to. Any limit here is not a limit imposed on God by us, but a limit God sovereignly imposes on himself.

In Reformed theology, if God is not sovereign over the entire created order, then he is not sovereign at all. The term *sovereignty* too easily becomes a chimera. If God is not sovereign, then he is not God. It belongs to God as God to be sovereign. How we understand his sovereignty has radical implications for our understanding of the doctrines of providence, election, justification, and a host of others. The same could be said regarding other attributes of God, such as his holiness, omniscience, and immutability, to name but a few.

Reformed Theology Is Catholic

In the seventeenth century a dispute arose in the Reformed community in Holland. A group of theologians became known as the Remonstrants because they remonstrated (protested) against five articles of Reformed theology. These five points later became known as the "Five Points of Calvinism," which have been summarized by the popular acrostic TULIP. This acrostic (which we shall examine more closely in part 2) stands for total depravity, unconditional election, limited atonement, irresistible grace, and the perseverance of the saints. The Synod of Dort condemned the Remonstrants and reaffirmed the five points as integral to orthodox Reformed theology.

Since this synod it has become increasingly popular to view Reformed theology exclusively in light of these five points. Although these five points may be central to Reformed theology, they by no means exhaust this system of doctrine. There is much more to Reformed theology than the five points.

Reformed theology is not only systematic but also *catholic*, sharing much in common with other communions that are part of historic Christianity. The sixteenth-century Reformers were not interested in creating a new religion. They were interested, not in innovation, but in renovation. They were reformers, not revolutionaries. Just as the Old Testament prophets did not repudiate the original covenant God had made with Israel, seeking instead to correct the departures from revealed faith, so the Reformers called the church back to its apostolic and biblical roots.

Though the Reformers rejected church tradition as a source of divine revelation, they did not thereby despise the entire scope of Christian tradition. John Calvin and Martin Luther frequently quoted the church fathers, especially Augustine. They believed the church had learned much in her history, and they wished to conserve what was true in that tradition. For example, the Reformers embraced the doctrines articulated and formulated by the great ecumenical councils of church history, including the doctrines of the Trinity and of Christ's person and work formulated at the councils of Nicea in 325 and of Chalcedon in 451.

In the New Testament itself we see a conflict concerning tradition. Jesus was frequently locked in controversy with the Pharisees and scribes over the tradition of the rabbis. Jesus did not regard the rabbinic tradition as inviolate. On the contrary he rebuked the Pharisees for elevating this human tradition to the level of divine authority, which compromised the latter. Because of this stern rebuke of human tradition, we tend to miss the positive aspects of tradition articulated in the New Testament. The term *tradition* here refers to that which is "given over." Paul speaks warmly of the gospel tradition in which he worked. It is the duty of every generation of Christians to pass on a tradition. Just as Israel was called to pass on to their children the traditions instituted by God, so the church is to pass on the apostolic tradition to each successive generation.

In this process, however, there is always the danger of adding accretions to the apostolic tradition that are contrary to the original. That is why the Reformers insisted that their work of reformation was not complete. The church is called to be *semper reformanda*, "always reforming." Every Christian community creates its own subculture of customs and traditions. Such traditions are often extremely difficult to overcome or abandon. Yet it remains our task in every generation to examine critically our own traditions to insure they are consistent with the apostolic tradition.

The Reformers took church history very seriously, and we should do the same today. I have taught systematic theology in Reformed seminaries attended by students from a variety of denominational backgrounds. When I teach the sacraments, I know many of my students are Baptists and do not embrace the doctrine of infant baptism. I point out to them that the practice of infant baptism is the majority position in church history among the majority of Christian communions. I remind them that, though theirs is a minority position historically, that by no means makes it false. Indeed, the minority may be and often is right. I do ask my Baptist students to examine the majority position to see why that tradition holds the view that it does. Likewise I insist that students who disagree with the Baptist position listen carefully to the case the Baptists make for believer's baptism.

I do this for more than one reason. This issue divides earnest Christians, both sides of which clearly desire to please God. At least one of these two groups is in error. The baptism of infants is either in accord with the divine will or it is not. Somebody is wrong, yet both believe they are right. By examining the historical debates on this issue, we may be persuaded to change our thinking. At the very least we will acquire a deeper understanding of the issues involved. This creates an environment of mutual understanding even in the midst of serious disagreement.

Reformed Theology Is Evangelical

The term *evangelical* came into prominence during the Reformation, when it was virtually a synonym for *protestant*. Historians have often suggested that the two chief causes of the Reformation were the issues of authority and justification. Frequently the issue of authority is called the Reformation's *formal cause*, while the issue of justification is called its *material cause*. By this is meant that the core issue was justification, while the backdrop to the controversy was authority. The twin slogans of *sola Scriptura* and *sola fide* became the battle cries of the Reformation. We will examine these two matters more fully later. We note them now in passing to say that the term *evangelical* was the broad term applied to many groups that, despite their separation into different denominations, agreed on these two basic issues over against the Roman Catholic church.

When we declare that Reformed theology is evangelical, we mean that Reformed theology shares with other Protestant groups a commitment to the historic doctrines of *sola Scriptura* and *sola fide*. Since the sixteenth century the term *evangelical* has undergone a significant development, so that today it is difficult to define. In the twentieth century both the concept of biblical authority and the nature and significance of justification by faith alone have been challenged from within the community of confessing evangelicals. It is no longer safe to assume that if a person calls himself an evangelical that he is committed to either *sola Scriptura* or *sola fide*.

In a recent book a Roman Catholic writer described himself as an "evangelical Roman Catholic" and affirmed his commitment to orthodox Romanism. He claimed the label evangelical because he too believes the "gospel." This author understands the root meaning of the term *evangelical*.

The Reformers called themselves evangelicals because they believed the doctrine of justification by faith alone is central and essential to the gospel. Since the biblical word for gospel is *evangel*, they used the term *evangelical* to assert their conviction that *sola fide* is the gospel. Of course the Roman church of the sixteenth century disagreed with the Reformers and argued that *sola fide* is a serious distortion of the gospel. In light of the historic debate, it is not surprising to find adherents on both sides of the issue calling themselves *evangelicals* today. (Of course it must also be acknowledged that there are people within the Roman Catholic church who are *evangelical* in the Protestant sense, believing the Reformation view of the gospel and not the Roman Catholic view.) In any case, when I say that Reformed theology is *evangelical*, I use the term in its classic and historical sense. Reformed theology shares a common, evangelical body of doctrines with other Christian communions.

God Is Incomprehensible

We have seen that Reformed theology is systematic, catholic, and evangelical. In all of these respects it seeks to be God-centered in its doctrine. When Reformed theologians confess their faith or teach courses in systematic theology, they usually begin the study of theology with either the doctrine of revelation or the doctrine of "theology proper," that is, the doctrine of the nature and character of God himself.

The study of theology proper normally begins with the doctrine of God's incomprehensibility. This term may suggest to the reader that we believe God is fundamentally unknowable or unintelligible. Indeed this is not the case at all. We believe Christianity is first of all a revealed religion. We are committed to the idea that God has made himself known to us sufficiently for us to be redeemed and to experience fellowship with him.

The doctrine of God's incomprehensibility calls attention to the distance between the transcendent Creator and his mortal creatures. One of the chief axioms taught by John Calvin was expressed by the Reformer in the Latin phrase *Finitum non capax infinitum*, "The finite cannot grasp (or contain) the infinite." Because God is infinite in his being and eternal, and we are finite and bound by both space and time, our knowledge of him is never comprehensive. We enjoy an apprehensive knowledge of God but not a comprehensive knowledge.

To know God comprehensively we would need to participate in his attribute of infinity. Infinity is a divine attribute rightly called "incommunicable," which means that God cannot make us gods ourselves. Even God is not capable of "creating" a second god. The second god could not really be a god because it would be by definition a creature. It would be dependent on and derived from the original God. Even in our glorified state in heaven, in which we will understand the things of God much more fully than we presently do, our knowledge of God will not be comprehensive. Our glorification does not mean deification. We will still be creatures; we will still be finite. Even in heaven the axiom applies: *Finitum non capax infinitum.*

Though we lack a comprehensive knowledge of God, we are not reduced to skepticism or agnosticism. We do apprehend God. The early church faced a virulent heresy in the form of so-called gnosticism. The gnostics, who derived their name from the Greek word for "knowledge" (*gnosis*), believed we can have no proper knowledge of God from the normal means of rational apprehension or the senses. The only channel of this knowledge is a mystical intuition possessed only by a gifted elite of *Gnostikoi*, or "those in the know." The gnostics claimed a superior level or type of knowledge to that of the apostles and sought to supplant their authority. The gnostic problem was exacerbated later with the rise of Neoplatonism.

Neoplatonism was a conscious attempt to provide an alternative philosophy to Christianity. The Christian faith having conquered traditional Greek philosophy, Neoplatonism was an attempt to restore Greek philosophy to preeminence. The most important Neoplatonic philosopher,

Plotinus, described God as "the One." Plotinus insisted that nothing positive can ever be affirmed about God. He is unknowable. We can circle around certain ideas about God, but we can never land on any of them. Plotinus popularized the method of speaking about God that is called the "way of negation" (*via negationis*), which defines something by saying what it is not.

Christian theology rejects the skepticism of gnosticism and Neoplatonism. The way of negation, however, is sometimes employed in theology. For example, we speak of God's infinity and immutability. Both are negative terms. To say God is infinite is to say he is not finite. To say he is immutable is to say he is not mutable, unchanging. In this respect we are pointing to dissimilarities between God and creatures. If there were only dissimilarities between God and man, we could have no knowledge of God at all.

It has become fashionable in our day to speak of God as being "wholly other." This phrase was coined to safeguard the transcendence of God against all forms of pantheism that seek to identify God with or contain him within the universe. If taken literally, however, the term "wholly other" would be fatal to Christianity. If there is no sense in which God and man are similar, if there is no analogy of being between God and man, then there is no common basis for communication between us. Utterly dissimilar beings have no way of discourse between them.

Scripture teaches that we are created in the image and likeness of God. This does not mean we are little gods. The image does not obscure the difference between God and man. It does assure, however, some point of likeness that makes communication possible, however limited it may be.

Though the church employs the way of negation in her statements about God, her confession is not, as in Neoplatonism, limited to this method. We also use the "way of affirmation" (*via affirmatas*) and the "way of eminence" (*via eminentia*). The way of affirmation makes positive assertions about God, such as "He is holy, sovereign, and just." The way of eminence describes God by elevating creaturely categories to the nth or ultimate degree.

For example, we are familiar with the categories of power and knowledge. We exercise power, but our power is limited. God's power over his creation is not limited; it is absolute. So we say God is all-powerful or omnipotent. Likewise, though our knowledge is limited, God's is not. We say that he is omniscient or all-knowing.

Our language about God takes into account both the similarities between him and us and the dissimilarities. The incomprehensibility of God seeks to respect that sense in which God is known by us and the sense in which he remains unknown to us.

Martin Luther distinguished between the "hidden God" (*Deus absconditus*) and the "revealed God" (*Deus revelatus*):

> A distinction must be observed when the knowledge or, more precisely speaking, the subject of the Divine Being is under discussion. The dispute must be about either the hidden *(abscondito)* God or the revealed *(revelato)* God. No faith in, no knowledge and no understanding of, God, insofar as He is not revealed, are possible. . . . What is above us is none of our business. For thoughts of this kind, which want to search out something more sublime, above, and outside that which has been revealed about

God, are thoroughly diabolical. We accomplish nothing by them except to hurl ourselves into destruction, because they propose an object to us that defies investigation, to wit, the unrevealed God. Let God rather keep His decrees and mysteries in hiding.[1]

John Calvin made a similar distinction between what we are able to know about God and what remains unknown to us. "His essence, indeed, is incomprehensible, utterly transcending all human thought; but on each of his works his glory is engraven in characters so bright, so distinct, and so illustrious, that none, however dull and illiterate, can plead ignorance as their excuse."[2]

Earlier Calvin extolled the knowledge of God that we do have: "Since the perfection of blessedness consists in the knowledge of God, he has been pleased, in order that none might be excluded from the means of obtaining felicity, not only to deposit in our minds that seed of religion of which we have already spoken, but so to manifest his perfections in the whole structure of the universe, and daily place himself in our view, that we cannot open our eyes without being compelled to behold him."[3]

Calvin and Luther, with the doctrine of God's incomprehensibility, sought to be faithful to scriptural teaching by holding to both aspects of the knowledge of God, his hiddenness and his self-revelation: "The secret things belong to the LORD our God, but those things which are revealed belong to us and to our children forever, that we may do all the words of this law" (Deut. 29:29).

We have already seen that Reformed theology is God-centered, not man-centered; theocentric, not anthropocentric. At the same time we realize that our understanding of God has radical implications for our understanding of humanity, which he created in his image. The knowledge of man and the knowledge of God are interrelated. They are bound up with one another. In one sense, by becoming aware of ourselves we become aware of our own finitude and creatureliness. We realize that we are dependent creatures. These things point us to the Creator, though in our fallen nature we seek to avoid or ignore this signpost. In another sense, it is not until we understand who God is that we adequately understand who we are.

In the very beginning of his classic work, *Institutes of the Christian Religion*, John Calvin says:

> Our wisdom, in so far as it ought to be deemed true and solid wisdom, consists almost entirely of two parts: the knowledge of God and of ourselves. But as these are connected together by many ties, it is not easy to determine which of the two precedes, and gives birth to the other. For, in the first place, no man can survey himself without forthwith turning his thoughts towards the God in whom he lives and moves; because it is perfectly obvious, that the endowments which we possess cannot possibly be from ourselves; nay, that our very being is nothing else than subsistence in God alone.[4]

Later Calvin turns his attention to the other side of the coin:

> On the other hand, it is evident that man never attains to a true self-knowledge until he have previously contemplated the face of God, and come down after such contemplation to look into himself. . . . So long as we do not look beyond the earth, we are quite pleased with

our own righteousness, wisdom, and virtue; we address ourselves in the most flattering terms, and seem only less than demigods. But should we once begin to raise our thoughts to God, and reflect what kind of Being he is, and how absolute the perfection of that righteousness, and wisdom, and virtue, to which, as a standard, we are bound to be conformed, what formerly delighted us by its false show of righteousness, will become polluted with the greatest iniquity; what strangely imposed upon us under the name of wisdom, will disgust by its extreme folly; and what presented the appearance of virtuous energy, will be condemned as the most miserable impotence. So far are those qualities in us, which seem most perfect, from corresponding to the divine purity.[5]

God Is Self-Sufficient

Reformed theology places great emphasis on God's self-sufficiency. This characteristic is related to God's *aseity*, the idea that God and God alone is the ground of his own being. He derives his being from nothing outside of himself. He is self-existent. In popular language we frequently refer to God as the Supreme Being and to ourselves as human beings. The word *being* appears in both designations. We might conclude that the fundamental difference between God and man is found in the adjectives *supreme* and *human*. In one sense this is correct.

But these adjectives point to the difference between the being of God and the being of man. God and God alone is pure being. He is who he is, the Yahweh of the Old Testament. Our being, by contrast, is derived, dependent, and contingent. We depend on the power of God's being for us to exist or to "be" at all. In a word, we are creatures. By definition a creature owes its existence to another.

One of my favorite anecdotes concerning God's self-existence is a conversation between two children. The first child asks, "Where do trees come from?"

The second child replies, "God made the trees."

"Where did we come from?"

"God made us."

"Well then," the first child asks, "where did God come from?"

Immediately the second child answers, "God made himself."

The second child's first two answers were fine. It was his third answer that got him in theological hot water. God did not make himself. Even God cannot make himself because this would require that he was already there to do the job. The very point of aseity is that God is not made. He has no prior cause. Because he has aseity, self-existence, God is eternal. There never was a time when he was not. He has the very power of being within himself. He not only has being, he is Being.

One Reformed confession, *The Westminster Confession of Faith*, says of God: "God hath all life, glory, goodness, blessedness, in and of Himself; and is alone in and unto Himself all-sufficient, not standing in need of any creatures which He hath made, nor deriving any glory from them, but only manifesting His own glory in, by, unto, and upon them. He is the alone fountain of all being, of whom, through whom, and to whom are all things; and hath most sovereign dominion over them, to do by them, for them, or upon them whatsoever Himself pleaseth."[6]

God Is Holy

Reformed theology attaches great importance to the Old Testament and its relevance to the Christian life. One of the Old Testament's great values is its rich revelation of God's character. Since Reformed theology places so much emphasis on the doctrine of God, it is not at all surprising that it pays so much attention to the Old Testament. To be sure, all of Scripture reveals the divine character to us. Yet the Old Testament provides a vivid portrait of God's majesty and holiness.

God's holiness refers to two distinct but related ideas. First the term *holy* calls attention to God's "otherness," the sense in which he is different from and higher than we are. It calls attention to his greatness and his transcendent glory. The second meaning of holiness has to do with God's purity. The perfection of his righteousness is displayed in his holiness.

Running through the works of the great theologians—like Augustine, Thomas Aquinas, Martin Luther, John Calvin, John Owen, and Jonathan Edwards—is the grand theme of the majesty of God. These men stood in awe before his holiness. This posture of reverence and adoration is found throughout the pages of Scripture itself. Calvin writes:

> Hence that dread and amazement with which, as Scripture uniformly relates, holy men were struck and overwhelmed whenever they beheld the presence of God. When we see those who previously stood firm and secure so quaking with terror, that the fear of death takes hold of them, nay, they are, in a manner, swallowed up and annihilated, the

inference to be drawn is, that men are never duly touched and impressed with a conviction of their insignificance, until they have contrasted themselves with the majesty of God. Frequent examples of this consternation occur both in the Book of Judges and the Prophetical Writings [Judg. 13:22; Isa. 6:5; Ezek. 1:28; 3:14; Job 9:4; Gen. 18:27; 1 Kings 19:18]; so much so, that it was a common expression among the people of God, "We shall die, for we have seen the Lord."[7]

I know of no other brief statement that so captures the central importance to theology of the doctrine of God. It is said that the driving passion of Calvin's theology and work in the church was to free the church from all forms of idolatry. Calvin understood that idolatry is not limited to crass or primitive forms like those found in animistic or totemic religions. He realized that idolatry can become subtle and sophisticated. The very essence of idolatry involves the distortion of God's character.

As Paul declared to the Romans, idolatry consists in exchanging the glory of God for a lie, elevating the creature and denigrating the Creator. Paul says: "Professing to be wise, they became fools, and changed the glory of the incorruptible God into an image made like corruptible man—and birds and four-footed beasts and creeping things. Therefore God also gave them up to uncleanness, in the lusts of their hearts, to dishonor their bodies among themselves, who exchanged the truth of God for the lie, and worshiped and served the creature rather than the Creator, who is blessed forever. Amen" (Rom. 1:22–25).

Calling the human heart an idol factory (*fabricum idolarum*), Calvin stressed that the propensity for idolatry is deeply rooted in the heart of sinful humanity. The exchange of the truth about God for a lie occurs in every distortion of God's character that creeps (or perhaps rushes) into our theology. It is a thing to be jealously guarded against. Calvin writes:

> Bright, however, as is the manifestation which God gives both of himself and his immortal kingdom in the mirror of his works, so great is our stupidity, so dull are we in regard to these bright manifestations, that we derive no benefit from them. . . . But we are all alike in this, that we substitute monstrous fictions for the one living and true God. . . . Almost every man has had his own god. To the darkness of ignorance have been added presumption and wantonness, and hence there is scarcely an individual to be found without some idol or phantom as a substitute for Deity. Like water gushing forth from a large and copious spring, immense crowds of gods have issued from the human mind, every man giving himself full license, and devising some peculiar form of divinity, to meet his own views.[8]

Christians are called to preach, teach, and believe the whole counsel of God. Any distortion of the character of God poisons the rest of our theology. The ultimate form of idolatry is humanism, which regards man as the measure of all things. Man is the primary concern, the central focus, the dominant motif of all forms of humanism. Its influence is so strong and pervasive that it seeks to infiltrate Christian theology at every point. Only by a rigorous attention and devotion to the biblical doctrine of God will we be able to keep from tasting and even swallowing this noxious brew.

2

BASED ON
GOD'S WORD ALONE

"Unless I am convinced by Sacred Scripture or by evident reason, I will not recant. My conscience is held captive by the Word of God and to act against conscience is neither right nor safe." These immortal words were uttered by Martin Luther at the Diet of Worms. He was on trial for his life before the authorities of both church and state, charged with serious heresy. When commanded to recant his doctrine of justification by faith, he insisted that his doctrine was based on the Bible. In earlier debates with leading Roman Catholic theologians, Luther had been maneuvered into admitting that he thought it possible for both the Pope and church councils to err.

Historians have frequently explained the Protestant Reformation by describing its material cause and its formal cause. Its material cause was the dispute over the doctrine of justification by faith alone (*sola fide*); its formal cause, the dispute over biblical authority (*sola Scriptura*).

Table 2.1
The Second Foundation Stone

1	Centered on God
2	**Based on God's Word alone**
3	Committed to faith alone
4	Devoted to Jesus Christ
5	Structured by three covenants

The principle of *sola Scriptura* lurked in the background throughout the debate over justification. Luther's refusal to recant at Worms brought it into the foreground. From that point on, *sola Scriptura* became a battle cry for Protestants.

The term *sola Scriptura* simply means "by Scripture alone." This slogan declared the idea that only the Bible has the authority to bind the consciences of believers. Protestants did recognize other forms of authority, such as church offices, civil magistrates, and church creeds and confessions. But they saw these authorities as being derived from and subordinate to the authority of God. None of these lesser authorities was deemed absolute because all of them were capable of error. God alone is infallible. Fallible authorities cannot bind the conscience absolutely; that right is reserved to God and his Word alone.

A common misunderstanding is that the Reformers believed in the infallible authority of Scripture while the Roman Catholic church believed only in the infallible authority of the church and her tradition. This is a distortion of the controversy. At the time of the Reformation, both sides acknowledged the infallible authority of the Bible.

The question was this: Is the Bible the *only* infallible source of special revelation?

Roman Catholics taught that there are two sources of infallible special revelation, Scripture and tradition. Since they attributed this authority to the tradition of the church, they did not permit any person to interpret the Bible in a way that was contrary to this tradition. That is precisely what Luther did, leading to his excommunication and the condemnation of his doctrine.

The Reformers agreed there are two kinds of divine revelation: *general* and *special*. General revelation, sometimes called *natural revelation*, refers to God's revelation of himself in nature. The apostle Paul declares this in Romans: "For the wrath of God is revealed from heaven against all ungodliness and unrighteousness of men, who suppress the truth in unrighteousness, because what may be known of God is manifest in them, for God has shown it to them. For since the creation of the world His invisible attributes are clearly seen, being understood by the things that are made, even His eternal power and Godhead, so that they are without excuse" (Rom. 1:18–20).

As we have seen, this revelation is called "general" because of both its audience and its content. All people receive God's revelation in nature; not all have read Scripture (special revelation) or been exposed to its teaching. General revelation does not reveal the history of redemption or the person and work of Christ; special revelation does.

Though the Reformers distinguished between general and special revelation, they insisted there is only one written source of special revelation, the Bible. This is the *sola* of *sola Scriptura*. The chief reason for the word *alone* is the conviction that the Bible is inspired by God, while church creeds and pronouncements are the works of men. These lesser works may be accurate and brilliantly conceived, capturing the best insights of learned scholars, but they are not the inspired Word of God.

The Inspiration of Scripture

The Reformers held to a high view of the Bible's inspiration. The Bible is the Word of God, the *verbum Dei*, or the voice of God, the *vox Dei*. For example, John Calvin writes:

> When that which professes to be the Word of God is acknowledged to be so, no person, unless devoid of common sense and the feelings of a man, will have the desperate hardihood to refuse credit to the speaker. But since no daily responses are given from heaven, and the Scriptures are the only records in which God has been pleased to consign his truth to perpetual remembrance, the full authority which they ought to possess with the faithful is not recognized, unless they are believed to have come from heaven, as directly as if God had been heard giving utterance to them.[1]

"As if" does not mean Calvin believed that the Bible had dropped down from heaven directly or that God himself wrote the words on the pages of Scripture. Rather "as if" refers to the weight of divine authority that attends the Scriptures. This authority is rooted and grounded in the fact that Scripture was originally given under divine inspiration. This claim agrees with the Bible's own claim to authority: "All Scripture is given by inspiration of God, and is profitable for doctrine, for reproof, for correction, for instruction in righteousness, that the man of God may be complete, thoroughly equipped for every good work" (2 Tim. 3:16–17).

Paul's declaration of Scripture's inspiration refers to its origin. He uses the Greek word *theopneustos*, which means "God-breathed." Though the word is usually translated "inspired," which means "breathe in," technically *theopneustos* refers to a breathing out, which might more accurately be translated "expired." Paul is saying that Scripture is "expired" or "breathed out" by God. This is not a mere quibble. It is obvious that for inspiration to take place there must first be expiration. A breathing out must precede a breathing in. The point is that the work of divine inspiration is accomplished by a divine expiration. Since Paul says that Scripture is breathed out by God, Scripture's origin or source must be God himself.

When Calvin and others speak of Scripture's inspiration, they refer to the way in which God enabled the human authors of Scripture to function so that they wrote every word under divine superintendence. The doctrine of inspiration declares that God enabled the human writers of Scripture to be agents of divine revelation so that what they wrote was not only their writing but in a higher sense the very Word of God. The origin of Scripture's content is found ultimately in God.

Much debate has raged concerning the exact mode or method of this divine inspiration. Some have contended for a mechanical inspiration or dictation, reducing the human authors to robotic machines or passive stenographers who merely recorded the words dictated to them by God.

But the Scriptures themselves make no such claim. The mode or precise manner of divine inspiration is not spelled out. The crucial point of the biblical claim to authority is that God is the source who breathes out his word. It is clear from a study of the Bible itself that the authors' individual styles remain intact. The inspiration of the Bible refers then to the divine superintendence of Scripture, preserving it from the intrusion of human error. It refers to God's preserving his Word through the words of human authors.

The Infallibility of Scripture

The Reformers were convinced that, because the Bible has its origin in God and was superintended by his inspiration, it is infallible. Infallibility refers to its indefectibility or the impossibility of its being in error. That which is infallible is incapable of failing. We attribute infallibility to God and his work because of his nature and character. With respect to God's nature, he is deemed to be omniscient. With respect to his character, he is deemed to be holy and altogether righteous.

Theoretically we can conceive of a being who is righteous but limited in his knowledge. Such a being could make mistakes in his utterances, not because of a desire to deceive or defraud but due to his lack of knowledge. His would be honest mistakes. At the human level we understand that persons may make false statements without telling a lie. The difference between a lie and a simple mistake is at the level of intent. On the other hand, we can conceive of a being who is omniscient but evil. This being could not make a mistake due to lack of knowledge, but could tell a lie. This would clearly involve evil or malicious intent. Since God is both omniscient and morally perfect, however, he is incapable of telling a lie or making an error.

When we say the Bible is infallible in its origin, we are merely ascribing its origin to a God who is infallible. This is not to say that the biblical writers were intrinsically or in themselves infallible. They were human beings who, like other humans, proved the axiom *Errare humanum est,* "To err is human." It is precisely because humans are given to error that, for the Bible to be the Word of God, its human authors required assistance in their task.

At issue in our day is the question of Scripture's inspiration. On this point some theologians have tried to have their cake and eat it too. They affirm the Bible's inspiration while at the same time denying its infallibility. They argue that the Bible, in spite of its divine inspiration, still errs. The idea of divinely inspired error is one to choke on. We shrink in horror at the notion that God inspires error. To inspire error would require either that God is not omniscient or that he is evil.

Perhaps what is in view in the idea of inspired error is that the inspiration, though proceeding from a good and omniscient God, is simply ineffectual to the task at hand. That is, it fails to accomplish its intended purpose. In this case another attribute of God, his omnipotence, is negotiated away. Perhaps God is simply unable to superintend the writing of Scripture with sufficient power to overcome the human authors' propensity for error.

Surely it would make more sense to deny inspiration altogether than to conjoin inspiration with error. To be sure, most critics of the Bible's infallibility take their axes to the root of the tree and reject inspiration altogether. This seems a more honest and logical approach. It avoids the impiety of denying foundational attributes to God himself.

Let us examine briefly a formula that has had some currency in our day: "The Bible is the Word of God, which errs." Now let us expunge some of these words. Remove "The Bible is" so that the formula reads: "The Word of God, which errs." Now erase "The Word of" and "which." The result is "God errs." To say the Bible is the Word of God that errs is clearly to indulge in impious doublespeak. If it is the Word of God, it does not err. If it errs, it is not the Word of God. Surely we can have a word *about* God that errs, but we cannot have a word *from* God that errs.

That the Scripture has its origin in God is claimed repeatedly by Scripture. One example already noted is found in Paul's Epistle to the Romans. Paul identifies himself as "a servant of Jesus Christ, called to be an apostle, separated to the gospel of God" (Rom. 1:1). In the phrase "the gospel of God," the word *of* is a genitive indicating possession. Paul is speaking not merely of a gospel that is *about* God, but of a gospel belonging *to* God. It is God's possession and it comes from him. In a word, Paul is declaring that the gospel he preaches is not from men or of human invention; it is given by divine revelation. The whole controversy over the inspiration and infallibility of the Bible is fundamentally a controversy about supernatural revelation. Reformed theology is committed to Christianity as a revealed faith, a faith that rests not on human insight but on information that comes to us from God himself.

The Inerrancy of Scripture

In addition to affirming the Bible's infallibility, Reformed theology describes the Bible as inerrant. Infallibility means that something *cannot* err, while inerrancy means that it *does not* err. Infallibility describes ability or potential. It describes something that cannot happen. Inerrancy describes actuality.

For example, I could score 100 percent on a spelling test. In this limited experience I was "inerrant"; I made no mistakes on the test. This would not warrant the conclusion that I am therefore infallible. Errant human beings do not always err. They sometimes, indeed often do, err because they are not infallible. An infallible person would never err simply because infallibility as such precludes the very possibility of error.

In our day some scholars have asserted that the Bible is infallible but not inerrant. This creates no small amount of confusion. As we have seen, *infallible* is the stronger of the two words.

Why then have these scholars preferred the word *infallible*? The answer is probably located somewhere in the emotive realm. The term *inerrancy* is frowned on in certain academic circles. It is loaded with pejorative baggage. The term is often associated with unsophisticated and unscholarly types of fundamentalism. On the other hand, the term *infallibility* has a history of academic respectability, particularly in Roman Catholic scholarship. People may reject the Roman Catholic view of infallibility, but they do not identify it with backwoods, primitive theology. Jesuits, for example, do not suffer from a reputation of unsophisticated scholarship. To escape guilt by association with anti-intellectual circles, some have retreated from the term *inerrancy* and taken refuge in the term *infallibility*. If in the process *infallibility* is redefined to mean something less than *inerrancy*, however, then the shift in nomenclature is a dishonest subterfuge.

Though both *inerrancy* and *infallibility* have been integral to historic Reformed theology, the modern controversy over the Bible's trustworthiness has led others to argue that the concept of inerrancy was not advocated by the magisterial Reformers, but instead was originated by scholastic or rationalistic theologians of the seventeenth century. Though it may be accurate to say that the term *inerrancy* came into vogue later, it is by no means accurate to assert that the concept is absent from the works of sixteenth-century Reformers. Let us note a few observations from Martin Luther:

> The Holy Spirit Himself and God, the Creator of all things, is the Author of this book.[2]

> Scripture, although also written of men, is not of men nor from men, but from God.[3]

> He who would not read these stories in vain must firmly hold that Holy Scripture is not human but divine wisdom.[4]

> The Word must stand, for God cannot lie; and heaven and earth must go to ruins before the most insignificant letter or tittle of His Word remains unfulfilled.[5]

> We intend to glory in nothing but Holy Scripture, and we are certain that the Holy Spirit cannot oppose or contradict Himself.[6]

St. Augustine says in the letter to St. Jerome. . . . I have learned to hold only the Holy Scripture inerrant.[7]

In the books of St. Augustine one finds many passages which flesh and blood have spoken. And concerning myself I must also confess that when I talk apart from the ministry, at home, at table, or elsewhere, I speak many words that are not God's Word. That is why St. Augustine, in a letter to St. Jerome, has put down a fine axiom—that only Holy Scripture is to be considered inerrant.[8]

It is clear that the concept of inerrancy was not a late invention. It is attested to in antiquity, not only in men such as St. Augustine, but in Irenaeus as well. Luther cites Augustine's view with manifest approval. The same approbation is found profusely in John Calvin's writings.

Clearly inerrancy and infallibility do not extend to copies or translations of Scripture. Reformed theology restricts inerrancy to the original manuscripts of the Bible, or the *autographa*. The *autographa*, the initial works of the writers of Scripture, are not directly available to us today.

For this reason many scoff at the doctrine of inerrancy, saying it is a moot point since it cannot be verified or falsified without access to the original manuscripts. This criticism misses the point altogether. We carry no brief for the inspiration of copyists or translators. The original revelation is the chief concern of the doctrine of inerrancy. Though we do not possess the autographs themselves, we can reconstruct them with remarkable accuracy. The science of textual criticism demonstrates that the existing text is remarkably pure and exceedingly reliable.

Suppose the normative yardstick housed at the National Bureau of Standards were to perish in a fire. Would we no longer be able to determine the distance of three feet with accuracy? With the multitude of existing copies, we could reconstruct with almost perfect accuracy the original yardstick. To restrict inerrancy to the original documents is to call attention to the source of biblical revelation: the agents who were inspired by God to receive his revelation and record it.

Reformed theology carries no brief for the infallibility of translations. We who read, interpret, or translate the Bible are fallible. The Roman Catholic church adds another element of infallibility by claiming it for the church's interpretation of Scripture, especially when the pope speaks *ex cathedra* ("from the chair" of St. Peter). Though this adds a second tier of infallibility, the individual Roman Catholic is still left to interpret the infallible interpretation of the infallible Bible fallibly. Whereas Protestants are faced with a fallible interpretation of the church's fallible interpretation of the infallible Bible, Catholics assume a double level of infallibility.

Table 2.2
The Canon

	Biblical canon	Biblical books
Roman Catholic view	infallible	infallible
Protestant view	fallible	infallible

What does the Bible's infallibility mean for the average Christian seeking to be guided by Scripture? If the final stage of receiving Scripture rests in our fallible understanding, why is the infallibility of the original documents so important? This is a practical question that bears heavily on the Christian life.

Suppose two people read a portion of Scripture and cannot agree on its meaning. Obviously one or both of them misunderstand the text. The debate between them is a debate between fallible people.

Suppose, however, that the text is clear and that neither person disputes its meaning. If one of them is convinced that the text is God's infallible revelation, then the question of whether he should submit to it is answered. If the other person is persuaded that the text itself (in its original transmission) is fallible, then he is under no moral obligation to be bound by it.

The Authority of Scripture

The issue of Scripture's inspiration and infallibility boils down to the issue of its authority. A famous bumper sticker reads as follows: "God says it. I believe it. That settles it."

What is wrong with this statement? It adds an element that is unsound. It suggests that the matter of biblical authority is not settled until the person believes the Bible. The slogan should read: "God says it. That settles it." If God reveals something, that revelation carries the weight of his authority. There is no higher authority. Once God opens his holy mouth, the matter is settled. This is axiomatic for Reformed theology.

The question of *sola Scriptura* is fundamentally one of authority. Here the supreme authority rests with the Bible, not the church; with God, not with man. This came home to me in a discussion with a former college roommate. We had lost contact with each other and had not seen each other for twenty years when we met again at a theology conference, where I was speaking on the topic of biblical authority. After the meeting we had dinner together and my friend said to me, "R. C., I don't believe in the infallibility of Scripture any more."

I asked him what he did still believe in from our earlier days. He said, "I still believe in Jesus as my Savior and Lord."

I indicated I was pleased to hear this, but proceeded to ask, "How does Jesus exercise his Lordship over your life?"

My friend, a bit perplexed by my question, asked, "What do you mean?"

"If Jesus is your Lord, then that means he exercises authority over you. How do you know how he wants you to live if not from the Bible?"

"From the teaching of the church," he replied.

Here was a "Protestant" who forgot what he was protesting. He had come full circle, jettisoning *sola Scriptura* and replacing it with the authority of the church. He placed the church above Scripture. This is not unlike what occurred in Rome. Though Rome did not deny Scripture's infallible authority as my friend did, she nevertheless in a real and critical sense subordinated Scripture to the church.

The subordination of Scripture was a burning issue among the Reformers. John Calvin said: "A most pernicious error has very generally prevailed—viz. that Scripture is of importance only in so far as conceded to it by the suffrage of the Church; as if the eternal and inviolable truth of God could depend on the will of men. With great insult to the Holy Spirit, it is asked, Who can assure us that the Scriptures proceeded from God[?] . . ."⁹

Calvin then reminds the reader that the Scriptures themselves (Eph. 2:20) declare that the church is established on the foundation of the apostles and prophets. He continues: "Nothing, therefore, can be more absurd than the fiction, that the power of judging Scripture is in the Church, and that on her nod its certainty depends. When the Church receives it, and gives it the stamp of her authority, she does not make that authentic which was otherwise doubtful or controverted, but, acknowledging it as the truth of God, she, as in duty bound, shows her reverence by an unhesitating assent."¹⁰

Calvin has in view here the debate over the canon of Scripture. The sixty-six books of the Bible together comprise the canon of Scripture. The term *canon* means "measuring rod" or "rule." The Reformers did not recognize the books of the Apocrypha (written during the intertestamental period) as part of the canon. Rome did include the Apocrypha in the canon. Questions of which books are to be included in the canon were debated in the early church. In the final analysis the church recognized the books that now comprise the New Testament.

Since the church was involved in this process, some have argued that the Bible owes its authority to the church's authority and is therefore subordinate to the church's authority. This is the point Calvin so vigorously disputes. He declares that the church "does not make that authentic which was otherwise doubtful or controverted" but acknowledges it as God's truth. Calvin argues that there is a big difference between the church's recognizing the Bible's authority and the church's creating the Bible's authority. The church used the Latin term *recepimus*, which means "we receive," to acknowledge that books of the Bible are what they already were in themselves, the Word of God.

Luther wrote in a similar vein to Calvin concerning the relationship between the authority of the Bible and the authority of the church: "It is not the Word of God because the church says so; but that the Word of God might be spoken, therefore the church comes into being. The church does not make the Word, but it is made by the Word."[11] Luther goes on to say: "The church cannot give a book more authority or dependability than it has of itself, just as it also approves and accepts the works of the fathers, but thereby does not establish them as good or make them better."[12]

Roman Catholics view the canon as an infallible collection of infallible books. Protestants view it as a fallible collection of infallible books. Rome believes the church was infallible when it determined which books belong in the New Testament. Protestants believe the church acted rightly and accurately in this process, but not infallibly.

This does not mean that Reformed theology doubts the canonical status of books included in the New Testament canon. Some Protestant theologians believe a special work of divine providence kept the church from error in this matter without imparting to the church any permanent or inherent infallibility.

The Reformed doctrine of *sola Scriptura*, then, affirms that the Bible is the sole written authority for the faith and life of God's people. We respect and submit to lesser ecclesiastical authority, but we are not bound by it absolutely as we are by biblical authority. This is the basis for the Reformation principle of *semper reformanda*, which indicates that reformation of the church is an ongoing process. We are always called to seek more and more to bring our faith and practice into conformity to the Word of God.

The Interpretation of Scripture

One great legacy of the Reformation is the principle of *private interpretation*. The Reformation effectively put the Bible into the hands of the laity. This was done at a great price, as some who translated the Bible into the vernacular paid for it with their lives. The right of private interpretation means that every Christian has the right to read and interpret the Bible for himself or herself. This does not give an individual the right to misinterpret or distort the Bible. The Bible is not a waxed nose to be twisted and shaped to fit one's fancy. With the right of private interpretation comes the responsibility of handling the Bible carefully and accurately. Nor does this right suggest that teachers, commentaries, and so forth are unnecessary or unhelpful. God has not gifted teachers for his church in vain.

The Bible is not to be interpreted arbitrarily. Fundamental rules of interpretation must be followed to avoid subjectivistic or fanciful interpretation, rules developed by the science of hermeneutics. The term *hermeneutics* is etymologically related to Hermes, a Greek god. Hermes was the messenger of the gods, corresponding to the Roman god Mercury. In mythology Mercury is often depicted with wings on his shoes to facilitate the delivery of messages with speed.

Hermeneutics prescribes the process by which we seek to understand a message. The Reformation established crucial rules of hermeneutics for interpreting the Bible. Perhaps the most crucial or central rule is the *analogy of faith*. This is the rule that Scripture is to interpret itself (*sacra Scriptura sui interpres*). We are to interpret Scripture by Scripture. If the Bible is the Word of God, then it is coherent and consistent with itself. God is not the author of confusion. He does not contradict himself. We are not, therefore, to set one part of Scripture against another. What is unclear or obscure in one place may be clarified in another. We are to interpret the obscure in light of the clear, the implicit in light of the explicit, and the narrative in light of the didactic.

At a technical level the science of hermeneutics becomes quite complex. The biblical scholar must learn to recognize different forms of literature within the Scripture (genre analysis). For example, some parts of the Bible are in the form of historical narrative, while others are in the form of poetry. The interpretation of poetry differs from the interpretation of narrative. The Bible uses metaphor, simile, proverb, parable, hyperbole, parallelism, and many other literary devices that must be recognized in any serious work of interpretation.

One of the Reformation's chief accomplishments is the principle of the literal interpretation of Scripture. This concept has suffered from serious misunderstanding, having often been equated with a naive or wooden literalism. The actual principle, called the *sensus literalis*, is that the Bible must be interpreted according to the manner in which it is written. *Literal* refers to the literary form of Scripture. Luther comments on this:

Neither a conclusion nor a figure of speech should be admitted in any place of Scripture unless evident contextual circumstances or the absurdity of anything obviously militating against an article of faith require it. On the contrary, we must everywhere adhere to the simple, pure, and natural meaning of the words. This accords with the rules of grammar and the usage of speech *(usus loquendi)* which God has given to men. For if everyone is allowed to invent conclusions and figures of speech according to his own whim . . . nothing could to a certainty be determined or proved concerning any one article of faith that men could not find fault with by means of some figure of speech. Rather we must avoid as the most deadly poison all figurative language which Scripture itself does not force us to find in a passage.[13]

The principle of literal interpretation was intended to put an end to a method that had become popular in the Middle Ages, the *quadriga*. This was a method of interpretation by which four distinct meanings were sought for each biblical text: the literal, moral, allegorical, and analogical. This led to excessive allegorization and obfuscation of the text. By contrast, *sensus literalis* was designed to seek the plain sense of Scripture and to focus on one meaning. Though a text may have a multitude of applications, it has only one correct meaning.

The principle of the *sensus literalis* is closely related to the *grammatico-historical* method of interpretation. This method focuses on the historical setting in which Scripture was written and pays close attention to the grammatical structure of the biblical text. In a broad sense this method means simply that the Bible is to be interpreted like any other book. Its revelatory nature does not make it unlike any other book in that regard. It must still be read like any other book. In the Bible verbs are verbs and nouns are nouns. The normal structure of literature applies. Again Luther comments:

> The Holy Spirit is the plainest Writer and Speaker in heaven and on earth. Therefore His words can have no more than one, and that the most obvious, sense. This we call the literal or natural sense. But that the things meant by the plain sense of His plain Word may also mean something further and different, and thus one thing signifies another, is more than a question of words and languages. For this is true of all things outside Scripture, since all God's works and creatures are living signs and words of God, as St. Augustine and all the teachers declare. But we should not on this account say that Scripture or God's Word has more than one meaning.[14]

3

COMMITTED
TO FAITH ALONE

The doctrine of justification by faith alone (*sola fide*) is the central affirmation of historic evangelicalism. It is a doctrine Reformed theology shares with many other Christian denominations. Though this doctrine is not unique to Reformed theology, there would be no Reformed theology without it. Martin Luther is attributed with saying that this is "the article with and by which the church stands, without which it falls" (*articulus stantis et cadentis ecclesiae*).[1] If Luther was correct, then his statement applies not only to the Lutheran church but to any church.

Luther had this to say about justification by faith alone: "This doctrine is the head and the cornerstone. It alone begets, nourishes, builds, preserves, and defends the church of God; and without it the church of God cannot exist for one hour. . . ."[2]

Table 3.1
The Third Foundation Stone

1 Centered on God
2 Based on God's Word alone
3 Committed to faith alone
4 Devoted to Jesus Christ
5 Structured by three covenants

Elsewhere Luther declared: "The article of justification is the master and prince, the lord, the ruler, and the judge over all kinds of doctrines; it preserves and governs all church doctrine and raises up our conscience before God. Without this article the world is utter death and darkness. No error is so mean, so clumsy, and so outworn as not to be supremely pleasing to human reason and to seduce us if we are without the knowledge and the contemplation of this article."[3]

The doctrine of justification deals with what may be the deepest existential problem a human being can ever face: How can a sinner, an unjust person, ever withstand the judgment of a holy and just God? As the psalmist put it, "If You, LORD, should mark iniquities, . . . who could stand?" (Ps. 130:3). The question is obviously rhetorical. No one of us could possibly stand because none of us is righteous. For an unjust person to stand in the presence of a just God, that person must first be justified.

The Reformation focused on the question, *How* is a person justified? Clearly justification involves a legal judgment by God, a declaration by him that we are just. Then the burning question becomes this: On what basis or grounds does God ever declare anyone just? Must we first become just inherently before God will make such a declaration? Or does he declare us just before we are in ourselves actually just? John Calvin answered the question this way:

> A man is said to be justified in the sight of God when in the judgment of God he is deemed righteous, and is accepted on account of his righteousness; for as iniquity is abominable to God, so neither can the sinner find grace in his sight, so far as he is and so long as he is regarded as a sinner. Hence, wherever sin is, there also are the wrath and vengeance of God. He, on the other hand, is justified who is regarded not as a sinner, but as righteous, and as such stands acquitted at the judgment-seat of God, where all sinners are condemned. . . . Thus we simply interpret justification, as the acceptance with which God receives us into his favour as if we were righteous; and we say that this justification consists in the forgiveness of sins and the imputation of the righteousness of Christ.[4]

We notice some crucial words in this citation from Calvin: *deemed, regarded,* and *as if.* To say we are deemed or regarded as righteous in God's sight is to say we are considered, reckoned, or counted righteous in his sight. This means, as Calvin notes, that we are treated by God "as if" we are righteous.

Forensic Justification

The Reformed doctrine of justification is often called *forensic justification.* The term *forensic* is frequently heard in criminal trials. We hear of forensic evidence and forensic medicine. The word *forensic* refers to legal declarations. Forensic justification means we are declared righteous by

God in a legal sense. The ground of this legal declaration is the imputation of Christ's righteousness to our account.

Luther captured the idea of forensic justification with his famous Latin phrase, *simul iustus et peccator*, "At the same time [simultaneously], just and sinner." Luther did not intend to affirm a contradiction. The two assertions, just and sinner, refer to the same person at the same time, but not in the same relationship. The person considered in himself remains a sinner, yet at the same time, by virtue of the imputation of Christ's righteousness, the person is considered just in the sight of God.

This concept has been sharply criticized by Roman Catholics as involving a "legal fiction." They object that it casts a shadow on God's integrity because he declares a person to be just or righteous when that person is in fact not righteous. For God to turn fiction into fact is for God to be involved in a kind of fraud. For Rome, God can pronounce or declare a person to be righteous only if that person first becomes and is actually righteous. Anything less than this is fiction.

If Rome were correct on this matter, then Luther and the Reformers would say that the gospel itself is a fiction. To be sure, if God were to declare a person just or righteous when that person possesses no righteousness whatever, then God would be implicated in fraud. Rome is correct in insisting that the justified person must *possess* righteousness. The question is, How does the sinner acquire the necessary righteousness? This is the heart of the Reformation controversy.

The Roman Catholic church has emphatically and repeatedly condemned the ancient Pelagian heresy (though many Reformed theologians have claimed that Rome never really escaped it). Pelagius denied the doctrine of original sin, claiming that Adam's sin affected Adam alone and nobody else. Pelagius argued that man can become righteous without the assistance of divine grace. He allowed that grace "facilitates" the attainment of righteousness but is not necessary for it to be achieved. We may become righteous without grace, though grace helps if we make use of it. In condemning Pelagius, Rome insisted that we cannot become righteous without grace.

For Rome the grace necessary for justification is twofold. In the first instance an atonement is required to satisfy the demands of God's punitive justice. That atonement is made for us, graciously, by Christ. On the cross Christ paid the debt required for our sins. For the full measure of Christ's work to be applied to us, however, something else must take place. For us to be justified we must first be made righteous. The idea of being "made" righteous is tied to the Latin word for justification, *iustificare*.

How then are we made righteous? The Roman Catholic doctrine of justification is complex. Let us summarize this view. Justification begins with baptism, the "instrumental cause" of justification. By this sacrament the grace of Christ's righteousness is infused into the soul. The baptized person is cleansed of original sin and is now in a state of grace. The person must cooperate with and assent to the infused grace in order to become righteous. The grace of justification is not permanent. It may be lost through the commission of mortal sin.

Rome distinguishes between *mortal* and *venial* sin. Venial sin is real sin but is less serious. Mortal sin is called *mortal* because it kills the justifying grace in the soul. Mortal sin destroys grace but not faith. A person can retain true faith and still not be justified.

When a person commits mortal sin and loses the grace of justification received in baptism, he or she can be restored to a state of justification by the sacrament of penance. This sacrament is described by Rome as "the second plank of justification for those who have made shipwreck of their souls." The sinner confesses his sin to a priest, makes an act of contrition, receives priestly absolution, and then performs "works of satisfaction" to be restored to a state of grace.

These works of satisfaction lay behind much of the controversy in the sixteenth century. The works of satisfaction procure for the penitent congruous merit (*meritum de congruo*). Congruous merit is not condign merit (*meritum de condigno*), merit so worthy that a just God is obligated to reward it. Congruous merit is rooted in grace and is not so virtuous as to impose an obligation on God. It is instead "congruous" or "fitting" for God to reward this kind of merit.

Martin Luther strongly rejected the concept of congruous merit:

> These arguments of the Scholastics about the merit of congruence and of worthiness (*de merito congrui et condigni*) are nothing but vain figments and dreamy speculations of idle folk about worthless stuff. Yet they form the foundation of the papacy, and on them it rests to this very day. For this is what every monk imagines: By observing the sacred rules of my order I can earn the grace of congruence, but by the works I do after I have received this grace

I can accumulate a merit so great that it will not only be enough to bring me to eternal life but enough to sell and give it to others.[5]

Luther's vehemence on this point must be understood against the backdrop of the Reformation struggle. It is fair to say that the whole firestorm was ignited by an aspect of the sacrament of penance. The indulgence controversy that provoked Luther's famous *Ninety-Five Theses* focused on the concept of works of satisfaction, a concept integral to penance. One work of satisfaction a penitent may perform is the giving of alms. To be sure, alms must be given in a proper spirit to be effective.

In the sixteenth century Rome embarked on a huge building project involving St. Peter's Basilica. The pope made special indulgences available to those who gave alms to support this work. The pope has the "power of the keys," which includes the power to grant indulgences for people who are in purgatory because they lack sufficient merit to enter heaven. The pope can draw on the treasury of merit and apply it to the needs of those in purgatory. This treasury includes merit amassed there by the saints. The saints acquired not only sufficient merit to gain entrance into heaven, but also a surplus for others who had not. This excess or surplus merit is achieved by performing works of supererogation, works that are above and beyond the call of duty, such as martyrdom.

Johann Tetzel scandalized Luther by his crass method (unauthorized by Rome) of peddling indulgences. Tetzel marketed indulgences with the ditty, "Every time a coin in the coffer rings, a soul from purgatory springs." He gave peasants the impression that one could purchase salvation for departed friends and relatives simply by giving alms, with or without the spirit of penitence. At this point in his life Luther himself was keenly interested in these indulgences. He expressed remorse that his parents were still alive, preventing him from insuring their entrance into heaven by securing indulgences for them. Instead he gave alms in behalf of his grandparents.

When Luther raised questions about Tetzel's methods, he began to reevaluate the entire system of indulgences, including the sacrament of penance itself. He attacked the whole system, paying special attention to the concept of performing works of merit of any kind, whether congruous or condign. He insisted that the only merit that can avail for the sinner's justification is the merit of Christ.

Rome agreed that the merit of Christ is necessary for salvation. Likewise Rome insisted on the necessity of grace and faith for justification. Often the difference between the Roman view of justification and the Protestant view is misstated. Some say Rome believes in justification by merit and Protestants believe in justification by grace. Rome believes in justification by works, while Protestants believe in justification by faith. Rome believes in justification by the church, while Protestants believe in justification by Christ. To state the differences this way is to radically distort the issue and to be guilty of gross slander against Rome.

The Roman Catholic church believes that grace, faith, and Christ are all necessary for the sinner's justification. They are *necessary* conditions, but not *sufficient* conditions. While grace is necessary for justification, it is not enough. Merit (at least congruous merit) must be added to grace.

Rome declares that faith is necessary for justification. Faith is called the foundation (*fundamentum*) and the root (*radix*) of justification. Works must be added to faith, however, for justification to occur.

Likewise the righteousness of Christ is necessary for justification. This righteousness must be infused into the soul sacramentally. The sinner must cooperate with and assent to this infused righteousness so that real righteousness becomes inherent in the person before he can be justified.

Missing from the Roman Catholic formula for justification is the crucial word *alone*. It is not an exaggeration to say that the eye of the Reformation tornado was this one little word. The Reformers insisted that justification is by grace alone (*sola gratia*), by faith alone (*sola fide*), and through Christ alone (*soli Christo*).

Justification by Faith Alone

To grasp the full significance of the issue of justification, we must turn our attention to the meaning of the Reformation doctrine of justification by faith alone. While Rome maintains that the instrumental cause of justification is baptism, the Reformers insisted the instrumental cause is faith. An instrumental cause is the "means by which" something takes place. For example, when a sculptor creates a statue, the instrumental cause of the sculpture is the sculptor's chisel. The chisel is the means by which the sculptor fashions his art out of the stone.

In our justification, faith is the means by which we are linked to Christ and receive the benefits of his saving work. By faith we receive the transfer or imputation of the righteousness of Christ. Faith is not only a necessary condition, it is a sufficient condition for Christ's righteousness to be imputed to us. Faith, true faith, is all that is required to be justified by the righteousness of Christ. Faith trusts in and lays hold of a righteousness that is not our own.

"Justification by faith alone" is merely shorthand for "justification by the righteousness of Christ alone." His merit, and only his merit, is sufficient to satisfy the demands of God's justice. It is precisely this merit that is given to us by faith. Christ is our righteousness. God clothes his filthy creatures with the coat of Christ's righteousness. This is the very heart of the gospel, expressed not only in the New Testament but in the Old as well.

We must possess righteousness in order to be justified. The question is, Whose righteousness justifies us? Are we justified by a righteousness that is inherent in us, or by somebody else's righteousness that is imputed to us? Luther and the Reformers insisted that we are justified by a righteousness that is not in us but outside of us (*extra nos*). Luther said this:

> [A Christian] is righteous and holy by an alien or foreign holiness—I call it this for the sake of instruction—that is, he is righteous by the mercy and grace of God. This mercy and grace is not something human; it is not some sort of disposition or quality in the heart. It is a divine blessing, given us through the true knowledge of the Gospel, when we know or believe that our sin has been forgiven through the grace and merit of Christ. . . . Is not this righteousness an alien righteousness? It consists completely in the indulgence of another and is a pure gift of God, who shows mercy and favor for Christ's sake. . . . Therefore a

Christian is not formally righteous; he is not righteous according to substance or quality. . . .[6]

The "alien righteousness" of which Luther speaks is the righteousness of Christ. This righteousness does not adhere *in* us; it is earned *for* us. The Reformers agreed, of course, that Christ dwells in the Christian and so does the Holy Spirit. The ground of our justification is not this indwelling, however, but the merit of Christ wrought in himself, not in us. It is the legal application of his righteousness to us by which we are declared just. This is no legal fiction because real righteousness is really imputed. There is nothing fictional about the righteousness of Christ.

Imputation is at the heart of the Christian faith. If imputation is fiction, then the atonement is fiction. Christ's cross was real, and the punishment he received in our behalf was likewise real. He was the Lamb of God who bore our sins. How did he do that? As was symbolized in the Old Testament, our sins are transferred to Christ by imputation, not by infusion. God counted Christ's suffering as worthy satisfaction for our guilt.

Our salvation rests not only in Christ's atoning death, but also in his life of perfect, active obedience. If to secure our redemption Christ only needed to make an atonement for us, he could have come down from heaven and gone directly to the cross. But he also had to fulfill all righteousness by submitting at every point to the law of God. By his sinless life he achieved positive merit, which merit is imputed to all who put their faith in him. Christ not only died for us but he lived for us as well.

The dispute between justification by the *infusion* of Christ's righteousness and the *imputation* of his righteousness is no tempest in a teapot. It makes all the difference in the world whether the ground of my justification rests within me or is accomplished for me. Christ fulfilled the law for me and gained the merit necessary for my justification. This is the ground not only of my justification but also of my assurance of salvation. If I must wait until I cooperate with the righteousness of Christ infused within me, to the degree that I become inherently righteous, I despair of ever attaining salvation. This is not gospel or "good news"; it is bad news.

I love the church. It is the body of Christ. It nurtures my soul and aids in my sanctification. But the church cannot redeem me. Christ and Christ alone can save me. The sacraments are precious to me. They edify and strengthen me, but they cannot justify me.

Saving Faith

When Martin Luther declared that justification is by faith alone, serious questions arose about the nature of saving faith. Rome appealed to James 2:24 to repudiate the Reformation doctrine: "You see then that a man is justified by works, and not by faith only."

At first glance it seems that the Bible could not repudiate the doctrine of justification by faith alone more clearly than this. Then we read Paul's words in Romans: "Where is boasting then? It is excluded. By what law? Of works? No, but by the law of faith. Therefore we conclude that a man is justified by faith apart from the deeds of the law" (Rom. 3:27–28).

On one hand, James says a man is justified by works and not by faith only. On the other, Paul says we are justified by faith *apart* from works of the law. The problem is exacerbated when we see that both James and Paul appeal to Abraham to prove their points.

Though both Paul and James use the same Greek word for "justify," they are not using it in the same sense. They are dealing with different matters. Paul is clearly expounding the doctrine of justification, making it clear that it is by faith, not works. He appeals to Genesis 15, where Abraham is counted righteous by God the moment he believes. Paul argues that Abraham was justified *before* he performed any works of obedience.

James appeals to Genesis 22, where Abraham offers Isaac on the altar. Here Abraham is "justified," but in another sense. The question James is addressing is found earlier in chapter 2: "What *does* it profit, my brethren, if someone says he has faith but does not have works? Can faith save him?" (James 2:14).

James is asking what kind of faith is saving faith. He makes it clear that no one is justified by a mere profession of faith. Anyone can say he has faith. But saying it and having it are not the same thing. True faith always manifests itself in works. If no works follow from faith, then the alleged faith is "dead" and useless. Abraham demonstrated his faith by his works. He "showed" he had true faith, thus "justifying" his claim to faith. Abraham's profession of faith is vindicated in his demonstration of his faith in Genesis 22.

Paul argues that Abraham was already justified before God in Genesis 15 because he had true faith. Abraham did not need to prove the authenticity of his faith to God. God is able to read the heart. We are not. The only way I can see another person's faith is by observing his works. John Calvin remarks:

> If you would make James consistent with the other Scriptures and with himself, you must give the word *justify*, as used by him, a different meaning from what it has with Paul. In the sense of Paul we are said to be justified when the remembrance of our unrighteousness is obliterated, and we are counted righteous. Had James had the same meaning it would have been absurd for him to quote the words of Moses, "Abraham believed God," etc. The context runs thus: "Was not Abraham our father justified by works when he had offered Isaac his son upon the altar? Seest thou how faith wrought with his works, and by works was faith made perfect? And the Scripture was fulfilled which saith, Abraham believed God, and it was imputed unto him for righteousness." If it is absurd to say that the effect was prior to its cause, either Moses falsely declares in that passage that Abraham's faith was imputed for righteousness, or Abraham, by his obedience in offering up Isaac, did not merit righteousness. . . . What then? It appears certain that he is speaking of the manifestation, not of the imputation of righteousness, as if he had said, Those who are justified by true faith prove their justification by obedience and good works, not by a bare and imaginary semblance of faith. In one word, he is not discussing the mode of justification, but requiring that the justification of believers shall be operative. And as Paul contends that men are justified without the aid of works, so James will not allow any to be regarded as justified who are destitute of good works.[7]

At issue here is the question of genuine faith. The Reformers taught that "justification is by faith alone, but not by a faith that is alone." True faith is never alone. It always manifests itself in works. Works that flow out of faith, however, are in no way the ground of our justification. They contribute nothing of merit before God. The only ground or basis of our justification is the merit of Christ. Nor is faith itself a meritorious work or the ground of our justification. Faith is a gift of God's grace, so it possesses no merit of its own.

Like James, Luther opposed antinomianism. Saving faith is not dead. It is a vital or living faith (*fides viva*). Live faith produces real works. If no works follow from our profession of faith, this proves that our faith is not alive, but is what Calvin called an "imaginary semblance."

Luther's *simul iustus et peccator* is open to misunderstanding if this point is not made clear. Though we are justified and counted righteous before we are righteous in ourselves and while we are still sinners, we are nevertheless sinners who are in the process of becoming righteous. Our sanctification *begins* the moment we have faith and are justified. We must remember that a justified person is a changed person. One who has real faith is regenerate and indwelled by the Holy Spirit. The effect of this change is not only necessary and inevitable, but immediate. If no fruit follows, then no faith is present. If no faith is present, then there is no justification.

For Rome justification is the result of faith plus works. In Reformed theology justification is the result of faith alone, a faith that always produces works. Antinomianism teaches justification by faith minus works. Reformed theology rejects both the Roman and the antinomian views.

Early Reformed theologians customarily distinguished among various elements or aspects of saving faith. For the most part they discerned three chief aspects known as *notitia*, *assensus*, and *fiducia*.

Noticia refers to the content of saving faith. Faith has an object. It is not empty or a faith in nothing. Christianity rejects the maxim, "It doesn't matter what you believe if only you are sincere." Though sincerity is a virtue, it is possible to be sincerely wrong and to put your faith in something or someone that cannot save. People can sincerely worship or have faith in idols. Such faith is repugnant to God and cannot save. Certain information must be known, understood, and believed in order to have saving faith. For example, we must believe in God and in the person and work of Jesus to be saved. This is the data (*notae*) of faith. Without belief in the essentials of Christianity, saving faith is absent.

In addition to this data or content, one must also assent mentally (*assensus*) to the truth of this information. Saving faith gives intellectual assent to the truth of Christ's deity, atonement, resurrection, and so forth. We do not believe in what we believe to be a myth. If we reject the truth claims of the gospel, we cannot be justified.

The presence of both *notitia* and *assensus* is still insufficient for justification. Even the devil has these elements. Satan is aware of the data of the gospel and is more certain of their truth than we are. Yet he hates and despises the truth of Christ. He will not rely on Christ or his righteousness because he is the enemy of Christ. The elements of *notitia* and *assensus* are necessary conditions for justification (we cannot be justified without them), but they are not sufficient conditions. A third element must be present before we possess the faith that justifies.

This element is *fiducia*, a personal trust and reliance on Christ, and on him alone, for one's justification. *Fiducia* also involves the affections. By the power of the Holy Spirit the believer sees, embraces, and acquiesces in the sweetness and loveliness of Christ. Saving faith loves the object of our faith, Jesus himself. This element is so crucial to the debate over justification. If a sinner relies on his own works or on a combination of his righteousness and that of Christ, then he is not trusting in the gospel.

Synthetic Justification

The Reformed doctrine of justification has been called "synthetic justification"; the Roman Catholic doctrine, "analytical justification." An analytical statement is true by definition. It is a tautology. "A bachelor is an unmarried man" is true by definition or by analysis, because the idea of "unmarried man-ness" is already contained in the word *bachelor*. The predicate adds nothing that is not already present in the subject. The same is true of the proposition "A triangle is a three-sided figure" and of the equation $2 + 2 = 4$.

A synthetic statement, on the other hand, does add information in the predicate that is not inherent in the subject. In the statement "The bachelor is bald," baldness is new information. Though all bachelors are unmarried men, not all bachelors are bald. Here an idea is added in the predicate that is not present in the subject.

How does this apply to theology? When we say the Roman Catholic doctrine of justification is "analytical," we mean that God declares the believer just because, under analysis, the person is just. God only justifies those who have already been made just. God only declares just those who are just. He adds nothing to their inherent righteousness to make them just. To be sure something has been added, the infused grace of Christ's righteousness. This addition did not effect righteousness, it only made it possible through the believer's cooperation.

In the Reformed view of justification, something is added to the predicate that is not found in the subject. There is a "synthesis" because of the addition of Christ's righteousness by way of imputation. God does not declare the sinner just because the sinner, considered in himself, is just. God deems him just because of what is added to his account, the merit of the righteousness of Christ.

Although justification is by *faith*, if considered from another angle it may be proper to say that justification is by *works*. Ultimately justification is by works in the sense that we are justified by the works of Christ. Here the word *by* has a different reference. Normally the word *by* refers to the instrumental cause of justification, which is faith. It is by faith that the merit of Christ is appropriated to us. When we say we are justified "by" works, then *by* refers to the works of Christ, the meritorious ground or cause of our justification. We can combine these two concepts by saying that we are justified by faith in the works performed in our behalf by Christ.

The Remission of Sins

Justification involves the forgiveness and remission of our sins. We commonly use the word *remission* in two ways. When a cancerous tumor shrinks or disappears, we say the cancer is in remission. When we pay a bill, we say we have remitted payment. The root of the word *remission* means "to send." We derive the words *mission* or *missionary* from this root. (The words *missive* and *missile* derive from the same root.) In a basic sense the remission of sins involves the sending away of sins. It is a kind of removal of sin from our account. In the remission of sins, God blots out our transgressions from the divine ledger and removes our sins from us. This remission is integral to divine forgiveness.

John Calvin says: "Justification by faith is reconciliation with God, and . . . this consists solely in the remission of sins. . . . For if those whom the Lord hath reconciled to himself are estimated by works, they will still prove to be in reality sinners, while they ought to be pure and free from sin. It is evident, therefore, that the only way in which those whom God embraces are made righteous, is by having their pollutions wiped away by the remission of sins, so that this justification may be termed in one word the remission of sins."[8]

The apostle Paul stresses this aspect of justification:

For if Abraham was justified by works, he has *something of which* to boast, but not before God. For what does the Scripture say? "Abraham believed God, and it was accounted to him for righteousness." Now to him who works, the wages are not counted as grace but as debt.

But to him who does not work but believes on Him who justifies the ungodly, his faith is accounted for righteousness, just as David also describes the blessedness of the man to whom God imputes righteousness apart from works: "Blessed are those whose lawless deeds are forgiven, and whose sins are covered; blessed is the man to whom the LORD shall not impute sin." (Rom. 4:2–8)

Here the apostle explains clearly how the remission of sin relates to imputation. He speaks of the blessedness that attends God's imputing Christ's righteousness to the believer. This is the positive aspect of imputation. He also speaks of the blessedness that attends God's *not imputing* something, namely our sin. This is the negative aspect. In justifying us God does impute something (the righteousness of Christ) and does not impute something (our sin).

Martin Luther summarizes the idea of remission of sins:

A Christian is at once a sinner and a saint; he is wicked and pious at the same time. For so far as our persons are concerned, we are in sins and are sinners in our own name. But Christ brings us another name, in which there is the forgiveness of sins, that for His sake sins are remitted and pardoned. So both statements are true: There are sins, for the old Adam is not entirely dead as yet; yet the sins are *not* there. The reason is this: For Christ's sake God does not want to see them. I have my eyes on them. I feel and see them well enough. But there is Christ, commanding that I be told I should repent, that is, confess myself a sinner and believe the forgiveness of sins in His name. For repentance, remorse, and knowledge of sin, though necessary, is not enough; faith in the forgiveness of sins in the name of Christ must be added. But where there is such a faith, God no longer sees any sins; for then you stand before God, not in your name but in Christ's name. He adorns you with grace and righteousness, although in your own eyes and personally you are a poor sinner, full of weakness and unbelief.[9]

The remission of sins is tied to the atoning work of Christ. In the atonement both propitiation and expiation are involved. *Propitiation* refers to Christ's satisfaction of God's justice, making it "propitious" for God to forgive us. Propitiation may be seen as a vertical act of Christ directed to the Father. At the same time, Christ is an *expiation* for our sins, removing or carrying away from us our sins. As the Lamb of God, Jesus is our sin-bearer, taking our sins away and bearing them for us. On the cross Christ fulfills what is symbolized both by the slain lamb of Old Testament sacrifices and by the scapegoat on whom the sins of the people are transferred. The scapegoat was not sacrificed but was sent into the wilderness to take far away the sins of the people. This action symbolized the remission of sins.

One Gospel of Christ

The controversy over the doctrine of justification in the sixteenth century focused on the nature of the gospel itself. Both sides understood that something essential to Christianity was at stake. The church must always struggle with errors, but this controversy involved an article that is both central to the gospel and essential to it.

The apostle Paul frequently admonishes and instructs Christians not to be quarrelsome, divisive, or combative.

He extols the virtues of patience, charity, and tolerance. Yet when it came to the gospel itself, this same apostle was uncompromising. He considered some things utterly intolerable, and one is the distortion of the gospel. He wrote to the church in Galatia:

> I marvel that you are turning away so soon from Him who called you in the grace of Christ, to a different gospel, which is not another; but there are some who trouble you and want to pervert the gospel of Christ. But even if we, or an angel from heaven, preach any other gospel to you than what we have preached to you, let him be accursed. As we have said before, so now I say again, if anyone preaches any other gospel to you than what you have received, let him be accursed. For do I now persuade men, or God? Or do I seek to please men? For if I still pleased men, I would not be a servant of Christ. (Gal. 1:6–10)

Here the apostle uses strong language to condemn the perversion of the gospel. He insists there is only one gospel. The gospel he belabors in his letter to the Galatians is the gospel of justification by faith. The Judaizers were corrupting that gospel by adding works to it. Twice Paul pronounces an apostolic curse on this distortion, using the Greek word from which we get the English word *anathema*.

At the Roman Catholic Council of Trent in the sixteenth century, Rome condemned the Reformed doctrine of justification by faith alone and declared it anathema. They did this because they were convinced that the Reformed doctrine was "another gospel," a distortion of the biblical gospel.

The Reformers believed that in condemning justification by faith alone, the Roman communion was in fact condemning the biblical gospel itself. If justification by faith alone is indeed the biblical gospel, then Rome, by condemning it, condemned herself. Although Rome has maintained a strong commitment to many essential truths of the Christian faith, at Trent she rejected the article on which the church stands or falls, and Rome therefore fell as a church.

In table 3.2 differences between the Roman Catholic and Reformed doctrines of justification are listed. The list is not exhaustive, but it reveals that the approaches are not only different but also systemic. The entire concept of salvation, including the role played by Christ and the role played by us, is different. The two views are fundamentally disparate and incompatible. Attempts to harmonize them are doomed to failure at the outset.

Table 3.2
Justification

Roman Catholic view	Reformed view
Instrumental cause: baptism	Instrumental cause: faith
Infused righteousness	Imputed righteousness
Inherent righteousness	Alien righteousness
Analytical justification	Synthetic justification
Grace plus merit	Grace alone
Faith plus works	Faith alone
Christ's righteousness plus ours	Christ's righteousness alone
No assurance of salvation	Assurance of salvation

The doctrine of justification by faith alone is relatively easy to grasp with our minds, but to get it firmly in the marrow of our bones and in our very bloodstreams we must be ever vigilant. It is easy to forget it or to allow its clarity to be obscured. Martin Luther made this observation:

There are few of us who know and understand this article, and I treat it again and again because I greatly fear that after we have laid our head to rest, it will soon be forgotten and will again disappear. . . . And indeed we cannot grasp or exhaust Christ, the eternal Righteousness, with one sermon or thought; for to learn to appreciate Him is an everlasting lesson which we shall not be able to finish either in this or in yonder life.[10]

4

Devoted to the Prophet, Priest, and King

Just as Reformed theology shares a common foundation with Catholic Christianity with respect to the doctrine of God, so also it shares a common faith with respect to the person and work of Christ. The great Christological councils of the fourth and fifth centuries, the Council of Nicea (325) and the Council of Chalcedon (451), form the historic basis of Reformed Christology.

In the early centuries the Son of God's relationship to God the Father was a hotly disputed issue. Monotheism is so important in the Old Testament that it was important for the church, while confessing its faith in Christ's deity, not to compromise historic monotheism.

Table 4.1
The Fourth Foundation Stone

1	Centered on God
2	Based on God's Word alone
3	Committed to faith alone
4	**Devoted to Jesus Christ**
5	Structured by three covenants

Serious heresies emerged that threatened the church's confession of Christ's deity. Two major heresies were based on the concept of *Monarchianism*. The term *monarch* in our language describes royalty. Originally, however, the word was more directly linked to its Greek origin. The word *monarch* is a hybrid composed of a prefix and a root. The prefix *mono* means "one." The root *arch* means "beginning" or "chief, ruler." When combined, *mono-arch* or *monarch* means "one or single chief or ruler." The idea of Monarchianism, therefore, refers to God as the one or single ruler.

The first type of Monarchianism to threaten the church was called *Modalistic Monarchianism*. This view was linked to an old form of pantheism that saw all of the world or reality as a mode or level of God's being. This view was popular in both gnosticism and Neoplatonism. The heretic Sabellius argued that Christ was of one essence with God but was a lower mode of being than God himself. As the rays of the sun share a common essence or substance with the sun but may be distinguished from the sun itself, so Christ shares the same essence with God but is not God.

In this modalistic schema, everything can be said to be a part of God's essence. His being "emanates" from the center of his pure being. The further from that center the emanation is, the less purely it manifests God. Inert matter such as rocks are distant from the core of divine being, while angels, demiurges, and other spiritual beings are closer to the core of divine being. Jesus is a spirit being or demiurge, close to the core of divine being, of the same essence or the same being, radiating or emanating from the divine being, but he is not the divine being. Jesus partakes of "divinity" but is not really God.

At the Council of Antioch in 267 the church rejected Sabellius and his formula that Jesus is *homo-ousios* with the Father. *Homo-ousios* means "of the same essence, substance, or being," so Sabellius was declaring that Jesus is of the same essence as God, but he was still lower than God in his modalistic order of being. In place of *homo-ousios*, the church declared that Jesus was *homoi-ousios*, "of similar or like substance." The church rejected the term *homo-ousios* because it was loaded with the gnostic idea of modalism.

The Council of Nicea

In the fourth century the church faced a new heresy cloaked in a different form of Monarchianism, called *Dynamic Monarchianism*. It was "dynamic" in that it involved a kind of movement or change. In this view Jesus was not eternal God, but he "became" God via adoption. This view was championed by the heretic Arius, who had been influenced by the teachings of Paul of Samosata and Lucian of Antioch.

Arius was jealous to preserve pure monotheism. He saw Christ as the most exalted creature, indeed the first creature made by God. Christ was created first and then he, as a creature, created the rest of the world. Arius appealed to biblical texts that refer to Christ as "begotten" and the "first-born of all creation." In Greek the term *begotten* means "to be, become, or happen." In biological terms, to have been begotten is to have a beginning in time. If Christ was begotten, then he must have had a beginning in time and is not eternal. If he is not eternal, then he cannot be God.

For Arius, Jesus is preeminent and exalted, but originally he was not God. He was adopted into the godhead by virtue of his perfect obedience, by which he demonstrates his "oneness" with the Father. He is "one" with the Father in purpose and mission, but not in being. Arius embraced the formula accepted earlier at Antioch, that Jesus is *homoiousios* with God, that he is "like" God.

Arius and his followers were condemned as heretics at the Council of Nicea in 325. The Nicene Creed declares that Jesus was "begotten, not made." Here Jesus was believed to be eternally begotten of the Father. The Greek word *begotten* was taken not in a biological sense or in any sense that implies Christ had a beginning in time. Rather the term *begotten* has a filial sense, calling attention to the Son's unique relationship with the Father. The New Testament refers to Christ as the "only-begotten" of the Father, the *monogenēs*, a term that emphasizes the singular, once-for-all relationship between the Son and the Father.

One of the most ironic developments at Nicea is the council's affirmation of the term *homo-ousios* as the new benchmark of Christian orthodoxy. Nicea declared that

Christ was coeternal and cosubstantial with the Father, using the term *homo-ousios*. Here the church declared that Jesus is not merely of like essence with the Father, but that he is of the same essence or substance with the Father.

At first glance it may seem that the church retreated to the position of Sabellius and fell into the ancient gnostic heresy. Nothing could be further from the truth. By affirming *homo-ousios*, the church was not embracing the modalistic heresy it had condemned in 267. It was instead so determined to proclaim the full deity of Christ that it was willing to risk the dangers implicit in the *homo-ousios* formula. By then the threat of Sabellianism had faded and the threat of Arianism was so pressing that the church chose to use a term she once rejected in order to stop Arianism in its tracks.

The doctrine of the Trinity was at stake. With the *homo-ousios* formula the church clearly affirmed both the Trinity and the unity of the Godhead. The council affirmed that the Father, Son, and Holy Spirit were coeternal and coessential.

The Council of Chalcedon

By the fifth century the church had to face a new threat. The Council of Chalcedon had to fight against heresy on two fronts. The full deity and humanity of Christ were being assaulted by both Eutyches and Nestorius. Eutyches developed what is called the *Monophysite* heresy. The Greek term *monophysite* comes from *monophysis*, which means "one nature or substance." Eutyches argued that Christ is one person with one nature. He attacked the idea that Jesus is one person with two natures, a divine nature and a human nature.

For Eutyches Jesus had neither a purely divine nature nor a purely human nature, but a single theanthropic nature, one that can be viewed as either a humanized divine nature or a deified human nature. It was a mixture of both deity and humanity, which in reality was neither.

Table 4.2
Christological Councils

	Council of Antioch	Council of Nicea	Council of Chalcedon
Year	267	325	451
Heretical theologian	Sabellius	Arius	Eutyches, Nestorious
Heretical theology	Modalistic Monarchianism	Dynamic Monarchianism	Monophysite Christology
Council's decision	Jesus is **homoi-ousios** with the Father.	Jesus is **homo-ousios** with the Father.	Jesus is truly man and truly God. His two natures are not mixed, confused, separated, or divided.

Nestorius, on the other hand, argued that only two persons can have two natures. Hence he maintained that Jesus is really two persons. What Eutyches blended together, Nestorius tore apart. He separated the two natures into two distinct persons.

At the Council of Chalcedon (451) the church declared that Jesus was truly man and truly God (*vere homo, vere Deus*). His two natures were not *mixed, confused, separated*, or *divided*. These four negatives established the borders that guarded against heresy. Both the Monophysite heresy of Eutyches and the separation heresy of Nestorius were rejected.

The council added to the four negatives a crucial statement that has served as the basis for much theological dispute ever since. This statement affirms that each nature retains its own attributes, meaning that in the incarnation Christ's divine nature retained all of its divine attributes while his human nature retained the attributes of humanity.

Since the fifth century all orthodox branches of Christianity have affirmed the Council of Chalcedon's formula. Historic Reformed theology has adhered strictly to Chalcedonian Christology. What was said earlier about Reformed theology's consistent application of the doctrine of God may also be said of Christology.

Reformed versus Lutheran

One of the great tragedies of the Reformation was the inability of the Lutheran and Reformed theologians to sustain a lasting unity in important areas of theology. The division between these two groups focused on a disagreement regarding the doctrine of the Lord's Supper. If we were to examine this debate closely, we would quickly realize that at the root this was not so much a sacramental issue as a Christological one.

Both Luther and Calvin rejected the Roman Catholic view of the Lord's Supper, the Roman doctrine of *transubstantiation*. This doctrine teaches that in the miracle of the mass the bread and wine are supernaturally transformed into the body and blood of Christ. This transformation, however, is unique. It is not complete because the changed bread and wine still look like bread and wine, taste like bread and wine, and smell like bread and wine. To the senses no change is apparent. Yet the church asserts that the bread and wine have become the veritable body and blood of Christ. The consecrated host is kept in the tabernacle on the altar and is acknowledged by the participants' genuflections. At times the participants elevate the host and give obeisance to it.

To explain the disparity between appearance and reality, Rome makes use of the concept of transubstantiation. Borrowing from metaphysical categories used by Aristotle, Rome distinguishes between an entity's substance and its *accidens*, an object's external, perceivable qualities. These qualities indicate what something appears to be on the surface. Beneath the surface or beyond the physical level is a thing's real substance, its very essence.

For Aristotle the accidens of an object always flow from its essence. A tree always has the accidens of a tree because the accidens flow out of the tree's essence or treeness. One cannot have the substance of a tree and the accidens of an elephant.

The mass actually involves a double miracle. The substance of the bread and wine are changed into the substance of Christ's body and blood while the accidens of bread and wine remain. The substance of Christ's body and blood are now present without the accidens of his body and blood, while the accidens of bread and wine are present without the substance of bread and wine.

Luther objected that this double miracle is frivolous and unnecessary. He insisted that the body and blood of Christ are truly present but that they are supernaturally in, under, and through the bread and wine. The bread and wine remain both in substance and accidens.

Luther was still left with the problem that the accidens of Christ's body and blood remain hidden to the senses. The Lutheran view is that Christ is present "with" (*con*) the elements of bread and wine. This view is often called "consubstantiation," though many Lutheran theologians reject this label.

Calvin also insisted on the real presence of Christ in the sacrament of the Lord's Supper. In dealing with those who reduced the sacrament to a mere symbol (a naked sign), Calvin insisted on the "substantial" presence of Christ. When debating with Lutherans, however, he studiously avoided the term *substantial*, which they may have understood to mean "physical." Calvin affirmed the term *substantial* when it meant "real," but rejected it when it meant "physical."

For Calvin the issue was Christological. He denied Christ's physical, localized presence in the Lord's Supper, because body and blood belong properly to his human nature, not his divine nature. For Christ's physical body and blood to be present at more than one place at the same time, his physical body would need to be omnipresent. The Lord's Supper is celebrated at the same time in many parts of the world. How can the physical body and blood of Jesus be in Geneva, Paris, and London simultaneously?

Calvin believed that the *person* of Christ can be and is omnipresent. But his omnipresence is in his divine nature in that omnipresence is a divine attribute. The Reformers believed that Christ is now absent from us in his body (which is in heaven), but that he is never absent from us in his deity. The New Testament speaks of Jesus's departure, his "going away" from us, when he ascended into heaven, yet it also declares that he is always with us, even to the end of the age.

When we looked at the doctrine of the incomprehensibility of God, we noted Calvin's axiom *finitum non capax infinitum*, "The finite cannot grasp [or contain] the infinite." The word *capax* can be rendered either "grasp" or "contain." With respect to God's incomprehensibility, *capax* is rendered "grasp." When applied to Christ's incarnation, it is rendered "contain."

Calvin thought that in the incarnation the second person of the Trinity assumed a human nature. His divine nature, though joined to a human nature, could not be contained within the latter's finite limits. Jesus's human body took up space and had measurable limits. We are not to think that in the incarnation God gave up his divine attribute of omnipresence. The full being of God was not contained within the finite limits of the body of Jesus. This would involve a radical mutation in God's very nature.

The Roman Catholic church had debated this question of "ubiquity." The term *ubiquity*, a synonym for *omnipresence*, is derived from the Latin *ubi* ("where") and *equos* ("equal"). Literally the term means "equal whereness." Part of the debate focused on how the human nature of Jesus could be in more than one place at the same time. The answer was the "communication of attributes" (*communicatio idiomata*), a doctrine asserting that in the incarnation some divine attributes were communicated to Christ's human nature. Though human nature considered in itself is not omnipresent, it can be made omnipresent via the communication of this divine attribute.

A similar idea was expounded by Thomas Aquinas with respect to the knowledge of Jesus. Thomas struggled with Jesus's statement to his disciples regarding the day and the hour of his return: "But of that day and hour no one knows," Jesus said, "neither the angels in heaven, nor the Son, but only the Father" (Mark 13:32). Jesus indicates that the Father knows something he does not know, the day and the hour of his return.

Thomas argued that Jesus really did know the day and the hour because, as the Son of God, he had the attribute of omniscience. The two natures of Christ are so perfectly united that anything the divine nature knows the human nature must know as well. Thomas explained Jesus's words to his disciples with his theory of "accommodation." Jesus accommodated himself by saying he did not know something that in fact he did know, because the knowledge was too high or too wonderful or too secret for his disciples to know it.

The glaring problem with Thomas's view is that it has Jesus saying something that is not true. Perhaps this could be excused by stretching the principle that truth must be spoken only to those to whom it is due (a principle used to justify lying to protect innocent people in warfare, as Rahab did). But it was unnecessary for Jesus to lie in order to keep the matter concealed or secret from his disciples. He could have simply said it was none of their business.

Thomas's explanation perhaps preserved his view of the incarnation, but it left the church with a serious question about Christ's integrity. To be sure, Thomas did not conclude that Jesus told a sinful lie, but it is difficult to avoid this conclusion if Jesus deliberately distorted the truth.

Unlike Thomas, the Reformers had no problem with the limits of Jesus's knowledge regarding his human nature. At times Jesus (like the prophets) displayed supernatural knowledge. He surely always told the truth. He was infallible, but not omniscient. The divine nature can communicate *information* to the human nature, which communication surely did take place, but it cannot communicate *attributes*.

At issue in both debates (the limits of Jesus's knowledge touching his human nature, and his limited physical presence) is the question of the incarnation as it was articulated at Chalcedon. Chalcedon sought to avoid any confusion or mixing of the two natures that would result in the deification of the human nature or the humanization of the divine nature. To have Jesus's physical body present at more than one place at the same time smacks of the Monophysite heresy. It indicates a kind of deification of the divine nature. To communicate divine attributes to the human nature is to deify the human nature.

According to Chalcedon, "Each nature retains its own attributes." Calvin understood this to mean that the divine nature stays divine in every respect and the human nature stays human in every respect. To be human is to be limited in time and space. Those who embrace the idea of the communication of attributes from the divine nature to the human nature argue that in this transaction nothing is lost (or unretained) by the human nature, but that something is added to it. The question remains, How does this addition to the human nature avoid the mixing and confusing of the two natures condemned by Chalcedon?

John Calvin saw in Martin Luther's view of the Lord's Supper a subtle form of Monophysitism. Lutheran theologians countered that Calvin's rejection of the communication of attributes involved him in Nestorianism, the separation or division of the two natures.

Calvin had no intention of separating the two natures of Christ. He wished not to separate them, but to *distinguish* them. When the New Testament speaks of Christ weeping, sweating, or being hungry, we see manifestations of Jesus's human nature. When he wept, sweated, or hungered, he was still in perfect unity with his divine nature, but the tears, sweat, and hunger were not divine. God does not weep, sweat, or get hungry. The God-man did weep, but he did so in his humanity, not in his deity. Likewise the God-man died on the cross, but his divine nature did not die. If God had expired on the cross, the very universe would have ceased to exist.

Even while rejecting any separation of Christ's two natures, Chalcedon certainly distinguished between them. Perhaps the most important distinction we must make is the one between a distinction and a separation.

With respect to the Lord's Supper, Calvin insisted that Christ, the God-man, is indeed ubiquitous and truly and substantially present, but he is present in his divine nature. Nor does the divine nature rupture its unity with the human nature when it is so present. The human nature of Christ is now in heaven. It is still perfectly united to the divine nature. Though the human nature is restricted to its local presence in heaven, the divine nature is not so restricted because it cannot be contained by the finite.

Imagine an eight-ounce glass. Can it contain an infinite volume of water? No. The glass can contain only eight ounces. To be sure, Christ is not a glass. His human nature has the fullness of God dwelling in him bodily, but that fullness is by no means contained within that vessel of humanity or limited to it.

Nor did Calvin mean to suggest that in the Lord's Supper we can commune only with part of Christ, his divine nature. When this nature is present, Christ's person is present. When we meet his divine nature, we meet with him. As we commune with his divine nature, we commune with the whole Christ because his divine nature is still united with his human nature. The spatial gap is bridged, not by the human nature's stretching to us, but by the divine nature's link to the human nature bringing him into communion with us.

Christ as Prophet

In the seventeenth century *The Westminster Confession of Faith* declared that "it pleased God, in His eternal purpose, to choose and ordain the Lord Jesus, His only begotten Son, to be the Mediator between God and man, the Prophet, Priest, and King, the Head and Saviour of His Church, the Heir of all things, and Judge of the world: unto whom He did from all eternity give a people, to be His seed, and to be by Him in time redeemed, called, justified, sanctified, and glorified."[1]

In this brief statement the Westminster Assembly of Divines summarized the mediatorial office of Christ. As Moses was the mediator of the Old Covenant, so Jesus is the mediator of the New Covenant. A mediator is a go-between for two or more parties. In our culture we customarily think of mediators as those who are called into labor disputes. They seek an end to conflict, peace in the midst of some type of quarrel. In a word, the chief task of the mediator is to bring about *reconciliation* where there is estrangement.

The biblical drama of redemption focuses on reconciliation, an end to the estrangement between God and people. The natural state of fallen humanity is one of enmity toward God. Our rebellion against his divine rule sets us in opposition to him. We provoke his anger, and his judgment is set against us. We are in desperate need of reconciliation. It pleased God the Father to take the initiative to end this perilous estrangement by appointing Christ as our Mediator.

Though we say Moses was the mediator of the Old Covenant, his work of mediation was not one of ultimate reconciliation. His chief mediatorial work was, as God's spokesman, to deliver the law to God's people when he formed them as a nation at Sinai.

Indeed Moses was not the only mediator of this covenant. Others filled that role to a lesser degree. There were three main offices of mediation: the office of prophet, the office of priest, and the office of king. Persons who occupied these offices were anointed by God for these functions.

The idea of "anointing" grows in significance in biblical history as the Old Testament looked forward to one who would be the supremely Anointed One. The title *Christ* means "One who is anointed."

Persons occupying the three offices of prophet, priest, and king were go-betweens. They were selected by God to be representatives. The prophet represented God, speaking to the people on God's behalf, mediating his word to the people. The priest represented the people, speaking to God on the people's behalf. (Most liturgies assign the minister a combination of prophetic and priestly roles. When he reads the Scriptures or preaches a sermon, he fills a prophetic role. When he prays for the people, he serves a priestly role.)

The office of king was also mediatorial. The king was not autonomous or ultimately sovereign. He was to represent the rule of God over the people. The king of Israel was himself subject to the King's law. He was accountable and answerable to God for how he conducted his office. The frequent conflict in the Old Testament between kings and prophets was provoked by the corruption of kings who sought freedom from the constraints of the King's law. The prophets spoke to those kings for God, calling them to repent and to submit to the ultimate King.

John Calvin developed the Reformed doctrine of the threefold office of Christ, to which the *Westminster Confession* would later allude. This "threefold office" (*munus triplex*) refers to the consolidation of the Old Testament roles of prophet, priest, and king in the person of Christ.

In Christ the office of prophet reaches its zenith. Christ exceeds the level of any prophet before or after him. He is both the object and the subject of biblical prophecy. For Old Testament prophets their chief subject matter was the coming of Christ. They foretold his birth, ministry, and atoning death. They looked forward to the Messiah, who would be God's anointed king, as well as the Savior of his people.

Jesus also filled the role of the prophet. At his baptism Jesus was anointed by the Holy Spirit. Later God announced from heaven that Jesus is his beloved Son and that the people should listen to him. He spoke the prophetic word of God, declaring that he said nothing on his own but only what the Father had commissioned him to say.

Jesus frequently used the same form of announcements used by Old Testament prophets. Prophetic oracles, for example, were divine pronouncements of either weal or woe. Jesus's denunciation of scribes and Pharisees was usually prefaced by the words, "Woe unto you." His pronouncements of God's favor and mercy were introduced by the words "Blessed are you," as in the Sermon on the Mount. The "woe" and "blessed" formulas employed by Jesus hearkened back to oracles pronounced by Old Testament prophets.

His first recorded sermon (Luke 4:18–21), given in a synagogue, was based on a prophetic text. Jesus read Isaiah 61:1–2, then began his sermon, "Today this Scripture is fulfilled in your hearing."

Jesus also engaged in prophetic predictions, such as foretelling the destruction of Jerusalem (Matt. 24:1–28).

If we were to analyze the content of Jesus's prophetic utterances, we would see that the bulk of material contained within them concerns Jesus himself. The chief and central motif of his prophetic teaching, however, is the impending kingdom of God. Most of his parables focus on this subject. At the beginning of his earthly ministry, Jesus echoed the preaching of John the Baptist regarding the coming kingdom, which required a fresh level of repentance. The long-awaited and foretold kingdom was now at hand and the people were unprepared for it; they were unclean.

The scandal of John's ministry was that he called, not merely Gentiles, but Israelites to be baptized, indicating that Israel was also unclean. John called the nation to prepare itself for the coming of its King. He served as the herald of that King and announced his arrival with the *agnus Dei*, "Behold! The Lamb of God who takes away the sin of the world!" (John 1:29).

Christ as Priest

In addition to performing the prophetic office, Christ also fulfilled the Old Testament priestly office. Again Jesus was both the subject and the object of priestly ministry. The Old Testament work of the priest centered mainly on two functions: offering sacrifices and prayers in behalf of the people. Jesus undertakes both of these tasks and takes them to their zenith. As the great High Priest, Jesus offers a sacrifice that is so efficacious, it is given once for all. It is not to be repeated. It does not need to be repeated because it is perfect in its efficacy. To repeat it would demean it and cast an ominous shadow on its value.

When we say Jesus is the subject of the priesthood, we mean he actively made an oblation for the sins of his people. He offered the supreme sacrifice in our behalf. The New Testament underscores the importance of understanding that Jesus made this sacrifice voluntarily. Though he was executed by the authorities, they had no power over him except what he willingly granted to them. He insisted that none could take his life from him but that he was laying down his life for his sheep.

Jesus was also the object of his priestly work. The offering he gave was not a bull or a goat, but himself. The animal sacrifices of the Old Testament had no intrinsic value to effect atonement. They were but shadows or symbols representing the ultimate sacrifice that would be made by Christ. His blood and his blood alone, not the blood of bulls and goats, can satisfy the demands of God's justice. His was the perfect sacrifice, the sacrifice of the lamb without blemish. In his sinlessness Jesus met the qualifications required by God for propitiation.

Jesus did not offer his sacrifice in the temple. His blood was not sprinkled on the earthly mercy seat. He did not enter the Holy of Holies inside Jerusalem. On the contrary, he was executed outside the city, beyond the confines of the Herodian temple. Yet he gave his offering *coram Deo*, "before the face of God," and was received in the heavenly sanctuary. He sprinkled his blood on the cross, yet this blood sacrifice was received in the heavenly Holy of Holies and was accepted there as the perfect atonement for sin.

That Jesus fulfilled the role of high priest puzzled the Jews of the first century. They thought of the high priest strictly in terms of the Old Testament, Levitical priesthood. Since Jesus was not from the tribe of Levi, how could he be qualified for the role of high priest? To answer this question the author of Hebrews appealed to a Psalm: "The LORD has sworn and will not relent, 'You are a priest forever according to the order of Melchizedek'" (Ps. 110:4).

The author of Hebrews recounts the episode of Abraham meeting Melchizedek. This enigmatic person is identified as the priest of Salem. His name, *Melchizedek*, means "King of righteousness," and *Salem* derives from the

Hebrew word for peace. Melchizedek receives tithes from Abraham and pronounces his blessing on the patriarch.

The author of Hebrews argues that, according to Jewish custom, the lesser is blessed by the greater and the greater receives tithes from the lesser. This means that Melchizedek is greater than Abraham. Then the author reminds the reader that Abraham was the father of Isaac, who was the father of Jacob, who was the father of Levi. Again in Jewish terms, the father is greater than the son, which makes Abraham greater than his great-grandson Levi. If Melchizedek is greater than Abraham, then it follows that Melchizedek is greater than Levi. All of this demonstrates that the Old Testament had two priesthoods, and the greater of the two was that of Melchizedek. When God appointed Jesus the great High Priest, he made him a priest, not after the order of Levi but after the order of Melchizedek, as the psalmist had prophesied.

In fulfilling his priestly office Jesus not only offered the supreme, atoning sacrifice for sin, but he also intercedes for his people. A strange contrast can be seen in the New Testament between the fate of Judas and the fate of Peter. Both men were disciples of Christ. Both betrayed him on the night before his death, and Jesus predicted both treacherous acts.

When foretelling Judas's betrayal, Jesus simply said to him, "What you [have to] do, do quickly" (John 13:27). When predicting that Peter would deny him, Jesus said to Peter, "But I have prayed for you, that your faith should not fail; and when you have returned to Me, strengthen your brethren" (Luke 22:32).

There was no question of Peter's future repentance and restoration. This had been insured by Jesus's intercessory prayer in Peter's behalf. Judas did not receive the same benefit. In his high-priestly prayer Jesus said: "While I was with them in the world, I kept them in Your name. Those whom You gave Me I have kept; and none of them is lost except the son of perdition, that the Scripture might be fulfilled" (John 17:12). "The son of perdition" clearly refers to Judas.

Jesus's priestly ministry of intercession is cited by the author of Hebrews: "Seeing then that we have a great High Priest who has passed through the heavens, Jesus the Son of God, let us hold fast *our* confession. For we do not have a High Priest who cannot sympathize with our weaknesses, but was in all points tempted as we are, yet without sin. Let us therefore come boldly to the throne of grace, that we may obtain mercy and find grace to help in time of need" (Heb. 4:14–16).

Christ's priestly ministry included not only the offering of himself as the perfect oblation for our sins and the perfect atonement to render satisfaction of divine justice, but also his prayers:

> So also Christ did not glorify Himself to become High Priest, but it was He who said to Him: "You are My Son, today I have begotten You." As He also says in another place: "You are a priest forever according to the order of Melchizedek"; who, in the days of His flesh, when He had offered up prayers and supplications, with vehement cries and tears to Him who was able to save Him from death, and was heard because of His godly fear, though He was a Son, yet He learned obedience by the things which He

suffered. And having been perfected, He became the author of eternal salvation to all who obey Him, called by God as High Priest "according to the order of Melchizedek. . . ." (Heb. 5:5–10)

Christ's intercessory work did not end with his earthly ministry. It continues perpetually in heaven. In his ascension Jesus was elevated to the role of King situated at the Father's right hand, and in his session at the Father's right hand Jesus continues to make intercession for us daily.

Christ as King

As King, Christ fulfills Old Testament prophecies of an eternal kingdom for David and his seed. In Christ the fallen booth of David is restored. In Reformed theology the kingdom of God has not been utterly postponed to the future. Though that kingdom has not yet been consummated, it has been inaugurated and is a present reality. It is now invisible to the world. But Christ has already ascended. He has had his coronation and investiture. At this very moment he reigns as the King of Kings and the Lord of Lords.

Jesus is enthroned at God's right hand, and all authority in heaven and on earth has been given to him. It is a profound political reality that Christ now occupies the supreme seat of cosmic authority. The kings of this world and all secular governments may ignore this reality, but they cannot undo it. The universe is no democracy. It is a monarchy. God himself has appointed his beloved Son as the preeminent King. Jesus does not rule by referendum but by divine right. In the future every knee will bow before him, either willingly or unwillingly. Those who refuse to do so will have their knees broken with a rod of iron.

At present the kingship of Christ is invisible. We as Christians live somewhat like Robin Hood and his merry men of Sherwood Forest. Robin and his cohorts were disenfranchised by wicked Prince John. But John was a usurper. The throne belonged to Richard the Lionhearted, who was absent from the realm while on a spiritual crusade. We do not want to push the analogy too far, nor do we want to identify the condition of the church in this world with a myth or legend.

Our King is not visibly present in his realm, but his reign is real. No usurper can snatch it out of his hands. We live in this world as outcasts, but we must remain loyal to our King, who has ventured into a far country. We await his return in glory, seeking to give him reality in his absence. Our mission is to bear witness to his reign, which he instructed us to do just moments before he departed for heaven.

John Calvin argued that the church's task is to make the invisible kingdom of Christ visible. The essence of the ministry of witness is to make manifest what is hidden to the eyes of men. Our King is also Prophet and Priest, perfectly fulfilling the role of mediator of a new covenant that was sealed by and in his blood.

5

NICKNAMED COVENANT THEOLOGY

Reformed theology has been nicknamed "Covenant theology," which distinguishes it from Dispensationalism. Dispensational theology originally believed that the key to biblical interpretation is "rightly dividing" the Bible into seven dispensations, defined in the original *Scofield Reference Bible* as specific testing periods in redemptive history.[1] Dispensationalism sought a key that would unlock the proper structure of biblical interpretation.

Every written document has a structure or format by which it is organized. Paragraphs have subjects and chapters have focal points. Reformed theology sees the primary structure of biblical revelation as that of covenant. This is the structure by which the entire history of redemption is worked out.

Table 5.1
The Fifth Foundation Stone

1	Centered on God
2	Based on God's Word alone
3	Committed to faith alone
4	Devoted to Jesus Christ
5	**Structured by three covenants**

In the mid twentieth century a small monograph was published by George E. Mendenhall of the University of Michigan. In this monograph, entitled *Law and Covenant in Israel and the Ancient Near East,* Mendenhall wrote of the startling archaeological discovery of documents from the ancient Hittite nation, documents containing treaties governing the relationship between certain kings (suzerains) and their vassals. These "suzerainty treaties" revealed a structure that Mendenhall found in documents of other Near Eastern nations, including the Scriptures of Israel.[2]

Later Meredith G. Kline comprehensively analyzed this treaty structure in two books, *Treaty of the Great King* and *By Oath Consigned.*[3]

One of these ancient covenantal treaties began with a preamble, followed by a historical prologue. Then terms or stipulations of the treaty were enumerated, with sanctions attached. The treaty was sealed with vows and ratified by a "cutting" rite. Copies of the treaty were deposited in a safe public place, and the treaty was periodically renewed and brought up to date. We will look briefly at how this structure and form are evident in the Old Testament.

Preamble

Like the Constitution of the United States, ancient covenant treaties began with a preamble. The preamble identifies the sovereign of the treaty. When giving the Decalogue to Israel, God said, "I am the LORD your God. . . ." (Exod. 20:2). God identified himself by the sacred name he had revealed to Moses out of the burning bush in the wilderness:

> And God said to Moses, "I AM WHO I AM." And He said, "Thus you shall say to the children of Israel, 'I AM has sent me to you.'" Moreover God said to Moses, "Thus you shall say to the children of Israel: 'The LORD God of your fathers, the God of Abraham, the God of Isaac, and the God of Jacob, has sent me to you. This is My name forever, and this is My memorial to all generations.'" (Exod. 3:14–15)

The sacred name, *Yahweh* in Hebrew, is introduced here and serves as God's covenant name. He is the same God who had appeared to Abraham, Isaac, and Jacob and who had made a covenant with them:

> And God spoke to Moses and said to him: "I am the LORD. I appeared to Abraham, to Isaac, and to Jacob, as God Almighty, but by My name, LORD, I was not known to them. I have also established My covenant with them, to give them the land of Canaan, the land of their pilgrimage, in which they were strangers. And I have also heard the groaning of the children of Israel whom the Egyptians keep in bondage, and I have remembered My covenant." (Exod. 6:2–5)

Historical Prologue

After the suzerain was introduced in the preamble to a Hittite treaty, a brief history of the relationship between him and his vassals was given, in which the benefits conferred by the suzerain were rehearsed. Likewise in the Old Testament when God enacted a covenant with his people or when the covenants were renewed, he mentioned his previous works among them. At Sinai God said, "I am the LORD your God, who brought you out of the land of Egypt, out of the house of bondage" (Exod. 20:2).

Two things must be noted in the preambles and prologues to covenants God makes with his people. First, God has a name. He is personal, not an abstract force or an amorphous "higher power." He is not only a supreme being, but also a personal being who enters into a personal relationship with his people.

Second, he acts for the benefit of his people. He is "a God who . . ." At Sinai he identifies himself as the God who had liberated Israel from slavery in the mighty act of the exodus from Egypt. The God of the covenant acts in history and has a history of relationship with his people. He is no deaf and dumb idol, but the very Lord of creation, and he intersects human history with his redemptive activity.

Stipulations and Sanctions

The stipulations of ancient suzerainty treaties were the terms of the agreement between the king and his vassals. In industrial contracts today, the employee's responsibilities are spelled out, along with the compensation and benefits to be provided by the employer. Both the employee and the employer have responsibilities to perform. The Hittite suzerain promised to use his army to protect his vassals, and the vassals agreed to pay him tribute money.

In the Old Testament, stipulations are the laws God gives to his people. The Decalogue, for example, contains the stipulations of the covenant made at Sinai. It is important for the Christian to understand that the context of God's law is that of covenant. The law of God is not an abstract list of moral rules. His law comes to us in the context of a gracious covenant entered into by a gracious God. His people are to obey his law because it defines a personal relationship between them and God. It anticipates Jesus's words to his disciples, "If you love Me, keep My commandments" (John 14:15). God's covenant with us is rooted in his love. We show our love in return by obeying the stipulations or laws of his covenant. When we look at the law, we should see him as its author and obey it because of our personal commitment to him.

Ancient Near Eastern treaties contained dual sanctions: benefits were promised to those who kept the treaty's terms or stipulations, and penalties were prescribed for those who violated these terms. The sanctions of Old Testament covenants were expressed as blessings and curses, as in the book of Deuteronomy:

> Now it shall come to pass, if you diligently obey the voice of the LORD your God, to observe carefully all His commandments which I command you today, that the LORD your God will set you high above all nations of the earth. And all these blessings shall come upon you and overtake

you, because you obey the voice of the Lord your God: Blessed shall you be in the city, and blessed shall you be in the country. Blessed shall be the fruit of your body, the produce of your ground and the increase of your herds, the increase of your cattle and the offspring of your flocks. Blessed shall be your basket and your kneading bowl. Blessed shall you be when you come in, and blessed shall you be when you go out. The Lord will cause your enemies who rise against you to be defeated before your face; they shall come out against you one way and flee before you seven ways. The Lord will command the blessing on you in your storehouses and in all to which you set your hand, and He will bless you in the land which the Lord your God is giving you. (Deut. 28:1–8)

In contrast to the blessings promised for obedience, curses were promised for disobedience:

But it shall come to pass, if you do not obey the voice of the Lord your God, to observe carefully all His commandments and His statutes which I command you today, that all these curses will come upon you and overtake you: Cursed shall you be in the city, and cursed shall you be in the country. Cursed shall be your basket and your kneading bowl. Cursed shall be the fruit of your body and the produce of your land, the increase of your cattle and the offspring of your flocks. Cursed shall you be when you come in, and cursed shall you be when you go out.

The Lord will send on you cursing, confusion, and rebuke in all that you set your hand to do, until you are destroyed and until you perish quickly, because of the wickedness of your doings in which you have forsaken Me. (Deut. 28:15–20)

Oaths and Vows

Treaties in the ancient world were enacted by swearing oaths and vows. We see something similar in marriage ceremonies when promises and pledges are sealed by sacred vows. These vows are witnessed by various authority structures, such as family, friends, and the state. Preeminently, however, these vows are witnessed by God himself. Witnesses are needed to make the vows public, not merely private, and to observe the solemn ritual of the marriage covenant.

In biblical covenants vows are especially important. They are to be made by appealing to God as the witness. Swearing by anything less than God himself is prohibited as an act of idolatry. *The Westminster Confession of Faith* sees sacred vows as so important to true religion that it devotes an entire chapter to the matter. This confession says:

> A lawful oath is a part of religious worship, wherein, upon just occasion, the person swearing solemnly calleth God to witness what he asserteth, or promiseth, and to judge him according to the truth or falsehood of what he sweareth.
>
> The name of God only is that by which men ought to swear, and therein it is to be used with all holy fear and reverence. Therefore, to swear vainly, or rashly, by that glorious and dreadful Name; or, to swear at all by any other thing, is sinful, and to be abhorred.[4]

The commandment against taking the Lord's name in vain is directed chiefly against taking frivolous or insincere vows in his name. Likewise, swearing by anything else is abhorrent because it is a thinly veiled form of idolatry. To swear by the grave of one's mother, for example, is to impute divine attributes to that site. The grave has no eyes or ears to observe the vow and is impotent to bring judgment against those who break it. To swear by God is to invite him to witness the promise and to exercise his judgment on all who break the vow.

Scripture takes the swearing of vows so seriously because it takes covenants so seriously. The very basis of our relationship with God is a covenant. The chief ethical difference between us and God is that we are covenant-breakers while he is a covenant-keeper. We live with hope and confidence because God has made promises to us that he has sealed with his own vow.

We see this most clearly in the covenant he made with Abraham: "And it came to pass, when the sun went down and it was dark, that behold, there was a smoking oven and a burning torch that passed between those pieces. On the same day the LORD made a covenant with Abram, saying: 'To your descendants I have given this land, from the river of Egypt to the great river, the River Euphrates . . .'" (Gen. 15:17–18).

This strange passage recounts a crucial moment in redemptive history. After God had promised blessings to him, Abraham asked, "Lord GOD, how shall I know that I will inherit it?" (Gen. 15:8). Abraham already believed God, but he asked the Lord for assurance. God instructed him to cut up several animals and place the pieces on the ground. After God put Abraham in a deep sleep, the phenomena of the smoking oven and the burning torch appeared, passing between the pieces. What is the significance of this?

In this ritual God himself was swearing an oath. He is represented by the theophany of burning objects that pass between the animal pieces. The symbolism is clear: If God fails to keep his promise, he will be torn asunder like the animals. "If I fail to keep my promise to you," God is saying, "may my immutable being suffer mutation, may my eternal glory be destroyed, and may my very deity be ruined." God swears by the highest thing he can: himself.

This event in Genesis is alluded to in Hebrews:

> For when God made a promise to Abraham, because He could swear by no one greater, He swore by Himself, saying, "Surely blessing I will bless you, and multiplying I will multiply you." And so, after he had patiently endured, he obtained the promise. For men indeed swear by the greater, and an oath for confirmation is for them an end of all dispute. Thus God, determining to show more abundantly to the heirs of promise the immutability of His counsel, confirmed it by an oath, that by two immutable things, in which it is impossible for God to lie, we might have strong consolation, who have fled for refuge to lay hold of the hope set before us. This hope we have as an anchor of the soul, both sure and steadfast, and which enters the Presence behind the veil, where the forerunner has entered for us, even Jesus, having become High Priest forever according to the order of Melchizedek. (Heb. 6:13–20)

Ratification and Deposit

After vows were made and oaths were sworn in the ancient world, covenants were ratified by a cutting rite. The drama of Genesis 15 includes such a rite. Another example is the rite of circumcision used to ratify the covenant between God and Abraham (and his descendants). Circumcision involved the cutting off of the male's foreskin of flesh. It symbolized both positive and negative sanctions. It symbolized the blessing of Abraham and his descendants being consecrated, set apart from the mass of fallen humanity to be God's chosen people. Circumcision also dramatized the penalty for covenant breaking. "If I fail to keep my covenant oath," the Jew was saying, "may I be separated from God's blessings even as my foreskin has been separated from my body."

The ultimate rite of covenant ratification was the ratification of the New Covenant by the blood of Christ. Jesus instituted this covenant in the upper room during the Last Supper, then ratified it the next day by pouring out his blood on the cross.

Table 5.2
**The Structure
of Ancient Covenants**

1	Preamble
2	Historical prologue
3	Stipulations
4	Sanctions
5	Vows
6	Ratification

Just as copies of Hittite suzerainty treaties were deposited in a public place for safekeeping, so God instructed Israel to place the tablets of stone in the mercy seat, which was housed first in the tabernacle and later in the temple. The ark of the covenant where the tablets were kept was also called the ark of the testimony: "You shall put the mercy seat on top of the ark, and in the ark you shall put the Testimony that I will give you. And there I will meet with you, and I will speak with you from above the mercy seat, from between the two cherubim which are on the ark of the Testimony, of all things which I will give you in commandment to the children of Israel" (Exod. 25: 21–22).

From time to time God's covenant with Israel was renewed, such as at Moab with the death of Moses and at Shechem with the passing of Joshua. On these occasions the historical prologue was brought up to date, rehearsing God's latest redemptive acts in behalf of his people.

Covenant of Redemption

The first covenant we consider in the scope of Reformed theology does not directly include human beings, but is nevertheless critically important. The *covenant of redemption* involves the parties who work together to effect human redemption: the Father, the Son, and the Holy Spirit. This covenant is rooted in eternity. God's plan of redemption was no afterthought, designed to repair a creation run amuck. With the eternal and omniscient God, there is no such thing as "plan B." God worked out his plan of redemption before creation and even before the fall, though he conceived this plan in light of man's fall and designed it to effect redemption from the fall.

The covenant of redemption demonstrates the harmony within the Trinity. Over against theories that pit one member of the Godhead against the other two, the covenant of redemption stresses the total agreement between the Father, Son, and Holy Spirit in the plan of salvation. This covenant defines the roles of the persons of the Trinity in redemption. The Father sends the Son and the Holy

oluntarily enters the arena of this world
He is no reluctant Redeemer. The Holy
work of Christ to us for our salvation.
ot chafe at doing the Father's bidding.
Father is pleased to send the Son and the Spirit into the
world, and they are pleased to carry out their respective
missions.

John 3:16 declares that God so loved the world that he
sent his only begotten Son into the world. The initiative
for redemption belongs to the Father. The Son willingly
subordinates himself to this sending. He delights in doing
the will of the Father. During his earthly ministry Jesus
often spoke of his willingness to carry out the Father's
purpose. He said that doing the Father's will is his "food"
(John 4:34), and it is said that Christ is consumed by zeal
for his Father's house (John 2:17). He promised his disciples that they would inherit a kingdom the Father had
prepared for them from the beginning (Matt. 25:34).

All of this points backward to eternity, to the unity of
purpose of all three members of the Trinity. Just as the act of
creation was a trinitarian work, so the work of redemption
is trinitarian: the Father sends the Son and the Spirit, the
Son accomplishes the mediatorial work of redemption in
our behalf, and the Holy Spirit applies the work of Christ
to us. All of these actions are necessary to fulfill the terms
of redemption, terms agreed upon in eternity.

Covenant of Works

The initial covenant God made with mankind was a
covenant of works. In this covenant, according to the

Westminster Confession, "life was promised to Adam; and in him to his posterity, upon condition of perfect and personal obedience."[5] It is important to note that a "condition" is attached to this first covenant. The condition is personal and perfect obedience. This is a condition of works, and this is the covenant's chief stipulation. Life is promised as a reward for obedience, for satisfying the condition of the covenant.

The stipulation of obedience indicates clearly that this covenant is not unconditional. God has given no blanket promise that all men will enjoy eternal felicity no matter how they respond to his law. Law is given at the beginning, and obedience to it functions as a stipulation for covenant blessing.

The *Westminster Confession* avers that the obeisance required in this covenant must be both perfect and personal. The idea of partial or imperfect obedience is excluded. Man is created in God's image and is given the ability and duty to mirror and reflect God's holy character. There is no room for the slightest transgression.

In Eden the penalty for violating the covenant's terms was death. This penalty was not limited to spiritual death, nor would the penalty's execution be delayed. Death is to be imposed on the very day the transgression occurred. That Adam and Eve did not die physically on the day of their first sin already displays God's mercy and grace.

In later Old Testament history a catalog of sins is defined by God as offenses requiring capital punishment. From the vantage point of the New Testament, this code of justice may seem harsh, requiring cruel and unusual punishment. In light of the covenant of works, however, the penal code of the Old Testament is quite merciful. Originally *all* sin was a capital offense. Every sin is an act of cosmic treason, violates the rightful rule of God, and insults his infinite glory and perfection. The original mandate is clear: "The soul who sins shall die."

Because we live in a fallen world where sin is universal, we easily forget the original terms of the very life we receive from our Creator. We spout adages such as "Nobody's perfect" and "Everyone is entitled to one mistake." The latter is the ultimate bogus entitlement program. God has never given any human being a title to sin. Even if he had given each of us a spiritual or moral mulligan, we would have used it up long ago. Nor must we take sin so lightly that we deem it a mere "mistake." It is a moral revulsion to the holy God, an act of unspeakable arrogance, that any mortal would deign to set his or her will in opposition to the will of the sovereign God.

When the *Westminster Confession* says our obedience must be personal, it is not distinguishing between personal and impersonal. Impersonal things have no capacity for moral obedience. A moral being is by definition a personal being with the ability to act volitionally. Rocks and logs do not violate God's covenant because they are not personal beings.

Personal obedience refers to individual obedience. The covenant of works had no provision for vicarious obedience, obedience to God's law by one person in behalf of another. That feature is introduced in the covenant of grace, which has vicarious obedience at its very core.

The names of the two covenants, one of works and one of grace, may be misleading. The names may give the idea that the original covenant lacks any element of grace. That God creates us and gives us the gift of life is already an act of grace. God was under no obligation to create anyone. Once created, we had no claim on God to enter into a covenant with us. God's promise of life on the condition of obedience has its origin in his grace. Even in the covenant of works the reward promised for obedience is *de pactio*. The reward is given, not because the works themselves, due to their intrinsic value, impose an obligation on God to reward them, but because God in his grace offered such a reward as part of an agreement. Theoretically God could have justly and righteously imposed an obligation on his creatures to obey his law without any promise of reward whatsoever. It is the creature's intrinsic duty to obey his Creator, with or without the prospect of reward.

Covenant of Grace

The *Westminster Confession* declares this about the covenant of grace: "Man, by his fall, having made himself incapable of life by that covenant, the Lord was pleased to make a second, commonly called the *covenant of grace*; wherein He freely offereth unto sinners life and salvation by Jesus Christ; requiring of them faith in Him, that they may be saved, and promising to give unto all those that are ordained unto eternal life His Holy Spirit, to make them willing, and able to believe."[6]

Table 5.3
Three Covenants

	Covenant of Redemption	Covenant of Works	Covenant of Grace
Parties	The Father, the Son, and the Holy Spirit	God and human beings	God and sinful human beings
Initiator	God the Father	God	God
Time	In eternity past	At creation	After the fall
Condition		Perfect obedience	Faith in Christ (who satisfied the condition of the covenant of works)
Reward		Life	Spiritual life
Penalty		Immediate death (physical and spiritual)	Spiritual death

Perhaps the chief difference between the covenant of grace and the first covenant, and the reason why it is called a covenant of grace, is that this covenant is made between God and sinners. The covenant of works was made between God and his unfallen creatures. Once that covenant was violated and the fall had occurred, mankind's only hope was rooted totally in grace.

Though the covenant of grace is different from the covenant of works, it cannot be totally separated from it. In one important sense the covenant of works remains intact. God still exercises his just judgment on lawbreakers. The second covenant is an addition to the first. It does not annul the first covenant. Sometimes the covenant of works is called the *covenant of creation*, which makes it clear that the first covenant was not restricted to Adam and Eve. The first covenant was made with them and with their progeny. All human beings are included in the creation covenant. We may ignore or reject that covenant, but we cannot escape it. We are all under the sanctions of the covenant of works, and we are in desperate need of a covenant of grace.

Also important to remember is that, the second covenant notwithstanding, the way of salvation is still tied to the first covenant. The covenant of grace, far from destroying the original covenant, actually makes it possible for the covenant of works to be fulfilled.

Though the gracious doctrine of justification by faith is the essence of the gospel, we ought not forget that our salvation is ultimately accomplished by the fulfillment of the covenant of works. This is achieved by the second Adam, Christ himself, who by his perfect and personal obedience fulfills the requirements of the covenant of works. What is so gracious about the covenant of grace is that God accepts Christ's obedience to the covenant of works in our place. He does for us what we are incapable of doing for ourselves. Where we have not been personally obedient, God accepts vicarious obedience. The personal obedience of Christ is accepted as a substitute for our personal obedience, and this is what makes the covenant of grace so gracious.

The covenant of grace is manifest in specific covenants God made, such as those with Abraham, Moses, and David. Those covenants are but expansions of the covenant of grace. The *Westminster Confession* observes:

> This covenant was differently administered in the time of the law, and in the time of the gospel: under the law it was administered by promises, prophecies, sacrifices, circumcision, the paschal lamb, and other types and ordinances delivered to the people of the Jews, all foresignifying Christ

to come; which were, for that time, sufficient and efficacious, through the operation of the Spirit, to instruct and
build up the elect in faith in the promised Messiah, by
whom they had full remission of sins, and eternal salvation; and is called the old Testament....

There are not therefore two covenants of grace, differ-
ing in substance, but one and the same, under various
dispensations.[7]

It is interesting that the *Westminster Confession*, written
in the seventeenth century, refers to "dispensations." This
was before the advent of the system of doctrine known as
Dispensationalism. In the confession the word *dispensa-
tion* means "a kind of stewardship or administration,"
which is far removed from the word's usage in classical
Dispensationalism. Reformed theology knows nothing of
different testing periods or different redemptive agendas
for Israel and the church.

The *Westminster Confession* makes it clear that in Reformed theology, the way of salvation in the Old Testament is substantially the same as in the New Testament.
Redemption is always through grace by faith. In the Old
Testament faith was directed forward to the promised
future Redeemer, while in the New Testament faith is directed backward to the redemptive work of Christ, which
has been accomplished in history.

PART 2

FIVE POINTS OF REFORMED THEOLOGY

6

HUMANITY'S RADICAL CORRUPTION

Total depravity is the first of Calvinism's famous five points. It is somewhat unfortunate that the doctrine is called "total depravity" because this name can be misleading. It has prevailed because it fits the familiar acrostic TULIP. Total depravity makes up the T of TULIP. The term is misleading because it suggests a moral condition of *utter* depravity. *Utter depravity* means a person is as wicked as he can possibly be. *Utter* suggests both total and complete corruption, lacking even in civil virtue.

The doctrine of total depravity, however, does not teach that man is as wicked as he could possibly be. For example, Adolf Hitler, who often serves as the paradigm of human evil, surely had some behavioral patterns that were not utterly base. Perhaps Hitler loved his mother and at times was even kind to her (a hypothesis that may not fit the likes of Nero).

Table 6.1
The TULIP's First Petal

1	Total depravity	Humanity's radical corruption
2	Unconditional election	God's sovereign choice
3	Limited atonement	Christ's purposeful atonement
4	Irresistible grace	The Spirit's effective call
5	Perseverance of the saints	God's preservation of the saints

The term *total depravity*, as distinguished from *utter depravity*, refers to the effect of sin and corruption on the whole person. To be totally depraved is to suffer from corruption that pervades the whole person. Sin affects every aspect of our being: the body, the soul, the mind, the will, and so forth. The total or whole person is corrupted by sin. No vestigial "island of righteousness" escapes the influence of the fall. Sin reaches into every aspect of our lives, finding no shelter of isolated virtue.

Perhaps a better term for the doctrine of total depravity would be *radical corruption* (the only antipathy I have to this designation is that it may be abbreviated by the initials R. C.). The word *radical* derives from the Latin *radix*, which means "root." To say that mankind is radically corrupt is to say that sin penetrates to the root or core of our being. Sin is not tangential or peripheral but arises from the center of our being. It flows from what the Bible calls the "heart," which does not refer to the muscle that pumps blood throughout our bodies but to the "core" of our being. Even the word *core* derives from the Latin word for "heart."

Jesus frequently described this condition with images drawn from nature. Just as a corrupt tree yields corrupt fruit, so sin flows out of a corrupt human nature. We are not sinners because we sin; we sin because we are sinners. Since the fall human nature has been corrupt. We are born with a sin nature. Our acts of sin flow out of this corrupted nature.

The apostle Paul, citing the Old Testament, summarizes the universal condition of sin:

What then? Are we better than they? Not at all. For we have previously charged both Jews and Greeks that they are all under sin. As it is written:

> "There is none righteous, no, not one;
> There is none who understands;
> There is none who seeks after God.
> They have all gone out of the way;
> They have together become unprofitable;
> There is none who does good, no, not one"
>   [Ps. 14:1–3; 53:1–3; Eccles. 7:20].
> "Their throat is an open tomb;
> With their tongues they have practiced deceit"
>   [Ps. 5:9];
> "The poison of asps is under their lips"
>   [Ps. 140:3];
> "Whose mouth is full of cursing and bitterness"
>   [Ps. 10:7].
> "Their feet are swift to shed blood;
> Destruction and misery are in their ways;
> And the way of peace they have not known"
>   [Isa. 59:7–8].
> "There is no fear of God before their eyes"
>   [Ps. 36:1]. (Rom. 3:9–18)

Here the apostle speaks of our being "under sin." We use figurative language with respect to human conditions. We say a diligent person is "on top of" his work, which means he has it under control. Conversely to be "under" things is to be under their control. When Paul speaks of our being under sin, he is using the same sort of language. To be under sin is to be controlled by our sin nature. Sin is a weight or burden that presses downward on the soul.

In bringing the whole human race before the tribunal of God, Scripture indicts us all without exception, save for Jesus. It says, "There is none righteous, no, not one." The qualifying phrase, "no, not one," makes it clear that the universal judgment is not hyperbole. It is a universal negative proposition, from which none are excluded. The absence of exclusions or exceptions is not technically absolute when we consider the sinlessness of Jesus. This text, however, does not have Jesus in his moral uniqueness in view. It is evaluating the entire human race apart from Jesus.

The text then moves in a remarkable way from the general to the specific. Not only does it say there is none righteous, but it says there is none who does good, no, not one. We are not considered unrighteous because the dross of sin is mixed together with our goodness. The indictment against us is more radical: in our corrupt humanity we never do a single good thing.

How are we to understand this? Is it not our daily experience that many good deeds are performed by pagan people? The Reformers wrestled with this problem and acknowledged that sinners in their fallen condition are still capable of performing what the Reformers called works of "civil virtue." *Civil virtue* refers to deeds that conform outwardly to the law of God. Fallen sinners can refrain from stealing and perform acts of charity, but these deeds are not deemed good in an ultimate sense. When God evaluates the actions of people, he considers not only the outward deeds in and of themselves, but also the motives behind these acts. The supreme motive required of everything we do is the love of God. A deed that outwardly conforms to God's law but proceeds from a heart alienated from God is not deemed by God a good deed. The whole action, including the inclinations of the doer's heart, is brought under the scrutiny of God and found wanting.

Alexis de Tocqueville said civic virtue is motivated by "enlightened self-interest." Such outwardly virtuous acts are motivated, not by a desire to please or honor God, but by a desire to protect our own interests. We may learn, for example, that there are circumstances where crime does not pay. We may obey legal speed limits to avoid a speeding ticket. We are restrained from sinning to our full potential by law, culture, and the prospect of conflict with other sinful people. On the positive side, we might even do "virtuous" deeds, but we are motivated by a desire for the applause of others. Here the opposite assumption, that certain "virtues" actually pay in this world, plays a role. Absent in both cases is the motive of a heartfelt love for God.

Original Sin

The condition of radical corruption, or total depravity, is the fallen state known as *original sin*. The doctrine of original sin does not refer to the first sin committed by Adam and Eve, but to the *result* of that first sin. Original sin is the corruption visited on the progeny of our first parents as punishment for the original transgression. Virtually every Christian church has some doctrine of original sin. Though liberal theology, deeply influenced by humanistic assumptions, often decries original sin, all the historic confessions include the doctrine. To be sure, the *degree* of corruption involved with original sin has been a perennial point of debate among theologians. The consensus of historic Christianity, nevertheless, is that the biblical view of the fall requires us to affirm some concept of original sin.

One of the most volatile controversies of the fourth century involved the doctrine of original sin. The combatants were the famous Bishop of Hippo, Aurelius Augustine, and the monk Pelagius. Pelagius took offense at Augustine's famous prayer, "Grant what thou commandest, and command what thou dost desire."[1] Pelagius disagreed that it is in any way necessary for God to "grant" what he commands of us. Pelagius assumed that moral responsibility always carries with it moral ability. It would be unjust of God to require his creatures to do what they are unable to do in their own power. If God requires moral perfection, then mankind must be able to achieve perfection. Though grace *facilitates* our quest for moral perfection, grace is not *necessary* for us to reach it.

Augustine argued that grace not only facilitates our efforts to obey God, but because of our fallen nature, grace is necessary. Before the fall, the requirement for moral perfection was already present. The fall did not change the requirement, but it did change us. What was once a moral possibility became, without grace, a moral impossibility. Augustine's view is rooted in his doctrine of original sin. As the debate escalated, Pelagius aimed his guns at this doctrine.

Denying original sin, Pelagius argued that human nature was created not only good, but incontrovertibly good. Human nature can be modified, but the modifications can be only accidental, not essential. This terminology again reflects Aristotelian categories, whereby the word *accidental* does not mean "unintentional" but refers to changes that affect only the surface of something, not its deepest essence. Sin does not change our essential moral nature. We may sin, but we remain basically good.

Let me mention parenthetically that the idea of mankind's basic goodness is a cardinal tenet of humanistic philosophy. It also pervades modern American evangelicalism if recent polls are at all accurate. In a Gallup Poll the overwhelming majority of professing evangelicals indicated their agreement with the proposition that people are basically good.

At the heart of Pelagius's concern in his debate with Augustine was a desire to protect the idea of man's free will. Man both obeys God and sins against him according to the activity of a free will. Adam was given free will, and his will was not affected by the fall. Nor was guilt or fallen corruption transmitted to Adam's progeny. According to Pelagius, Adam's sin affected Adam and Adam alone. There is no inherited condition of corruption known as original sin. Man's will remains entirely free and retains the capacity for indifference, meaning it is not predisposed or inclined toward evil. All men are born free of any predisposition to sin. We are all born in the same moral condition that Adam enjoyed before the fall.

Augustine, on the other hand, argued that sin is universal and that mankind is a "mass of sin" (*massa peccati*). Man is incapable of elevating himself to the good without the work of God's grace within. We can no more return ourselves to God than an empty vessel can refill itself with water.

Augustine is famous for distinguishing various moral states or conditions of man both prior to the fall and after it. Before the fall Adam had the ability to sin (*posse peccare*) and the ability not to sin (*posse non peccare*). He did not possess the inability to sin (*non posse peccare*) or the inability not to sin (*non posse non peccare*).

We struggle a bit with this language because the last condition, which describes Augustine's view of original sin, is spelled out with a double negative, *non posse non peccare*. To say that fallen man is unable not to sin means that we are able only to sin. We simply are unable to live without sinning. We sin out of a kind of moral necessity because we act according to our fallen nature. We do corrupt things because we are corrupt people. This is the essence of what it means to be fallen.

Table 6.2
Augustine on Human Ability

Before the fall	After the fall
The ability not to sin and the ability to sin	The inability not to sin

John Calvin followed Augustine in this view of human corruption: "This is the hereditary corruption to which early Christian writers gave the name of Original Sin, meaning by the term the depravation of a nature formerly good and pure . . . when it was clearly proved from Scripture that the sin of the first man passed to all his posterity, recourse was had to the cavil, that it passed by imitation, and not by propagation. The orthodox, therefore, and more especially Augustine, laboured to show, that we are not corrupted by acquired wickedness, but bring an innate corruption from the very womb."[2]

The issue of innate corruption spawned the controversy between Pelagius and Augustine. Pelagius was condemned at the Synod of Carthage in 418. Subsequent church councils reaffirmed the doctrine of original sin and repeated the denunciation of Pelagius's teaching. Even the Council of Trent in the sixteenth century made it clear that Pelagianism seriously distorts the biblical view of the fall.

Martin Luther wrote this about original sin: "According to the apostle and the simple sense of him who is in Christ Jesus, it is not merely the lack of a quality in the will or indeed merely the lack of light in the intellect, of strength in the memory. Rather it is a complete deprivation of all rectitude and of the ability of all the powers of the body as well as the soul and of the entire inner and outer man. In addition to this, it is an inclination to evil, a disgust at the good, a disinclination toward light and wisdom; it is love of error and darkness, a fleeing from good works and a loathing of them, a running to what is evil. . . ."[3]

The apostle of whom Luther speaks is Paul. Perhaps Luther had Romans in mind when he made this statement. In Romans 3:11 Paul declares, "There is none who seeks after God." On the surface this is a startling judgment. The

Bible frequently admonishes people to seek after God, yet it also teaches that in our fallen state none of us in fact does seek after God. The basic posture of unregenerate man is that of a fugitive. Our natural inclination is to flee from God. The first sin in Eden provoked the first flight from his presence, a flight to hide from God and his scrutiny. The sensation of nakedness was linked to the first awareness of guilt. Adam and Eve sought a covering for their shame, a hiding place from their guilt. This was the first episode of human cover-up, a veritable "Edengate."

We frequently hear evangelical Christians say that their non-Christian friends are "seeking God" or "searching for God." Why do we say this when Scripture so clearly teaches that no unregenerate person seeks after God? Thomas Aquinas observed that people are seeking happiness, peace, relief from guilt, personal fulfillment, and other such benefits. We understand that these benefits can be found ultimately in God alone. We draw the inference that, because people are seeking what God alone can supply, they must be seeking God himself. This is our error. In our fallen condition we desire the benefits that only God can give us but we do not want him. We want the gifts without the Giver, the benefits without the Benefactor.

Romans 3:12 declares that all have "turned aside" or "gone out of the way." Sinners are indeed "wayward" persons. Before believers were called "Christians" (a term of derision), they called themselves "people of the Way." Jesus also spoke about different "ways," one that leads to life and one that leads to destruction (Matt. 7:13–14). Since no one seeks after God while unregenerate, it is no surprise that we all turn aside or move out of the way.

We do not "find" God as a result of our search for him. We are found by him. The search for God does not end in conversion; it begins at conversion. It is the converted person who genuinely and sincerely seeks after God. Jonathan Edwards remarked that seeking after God is the main business of the Christian life.

Idolatry

Romans 3:18 concludes with the indictment of fallen humanity that "there is no fear of God before their eyes." Perhaps this is the most devastating effect of original sin. We who have been created in God's image and who were made to worship and revere our Creator have lost the capacity for holy reverence before him.

Nothing is more foreign to our fallen state than authentic worship. This does not mean we have ceased worshiping altogether. Rather it means we have become idolaters, transferring worship from God to something in the created order. Paul says:

> For the wrath of God is revealed from heaven against all ungodliness and unrighteousness of men, who suppress the truth in unrighteousness, because what may be known of God is manifest in them, for God has shown it to them. For since the creation of the world His invisible attributes are clearly seen, being understood by the things that are made, even His eternal power and Godhead, so that they are without excuse, because, although they knew God, they did not glorify Him as God, nor were thankful, but became futile in their thoughts, and their foolish hearts were darkened. Professing to be wise, they became fools,

and changed the glory of the incorruptible God into an image made like corruptible man—and birds and four-footed beasts and creeping things. Therefore God also gave them up to uncleanness, in the lusts of their hearts, to dishonor their bodies among themselves, who exchanged the truth of God for the lie, and worshiped and served the creature rather than the Creator, who is blessed forever. Amen. (Rom. 1:18–25)

This section of Romans describes the universal practice of idolatry. The background for the indictment is that God clearly reveals himself in nature, with the result that every human being knows there is a God. But the universal response to this revelation is to suppress it and exchange this manifest truth for a lie. We trade God's glory for the glory of creaturely things. The very essence of idolatry is to erect an altar to a substitute for God. The fear of God to which Paul refers is not the servile fear or dread one has for an enemy, but the awe that fills the heart with reverence and inclines the soul to adoration. Sinners do not adore God by nature. We are by nature the children of wrath who carry in our hearts a fundamental enmity toward God.

To be in the state of original sin is to be in the state Scripture calls the "flesh." This does not refer primarily to things physical, but to a condition of moral corruption. In the flesh we are not able to please God. Indeed we have no desire to please him. We are estranged and alienated from God.

If we ask unbelievers if they hate God, they would probably deny it categorically. Yet the Scriptures make it plain that there resides in the hearts and souls of unregenerate men a deep hatred for God. Love for God is not natural to us. Even in the redeemed state our souls grow cold and we experience feelings of indifference toward him. When we pray, our minds wander and we indulge in woolgathering. In the midst of corporate worship, we are bored and find ourselves taking peeks at our watches. How dissimilar this is to our behavior when we are in the company of those we dearly love.

Our natural lack of love for God is confirmed by our natural lack of desire for him. As a youth I was required to memorize *The Westminster Shorter Catechism*. To me this was an onerous task. The first question of the catechism is "What is the chief end of man?" The answer reads, "Man's chief end is to glorify God, and to enjoy him for ever." This did not make much sense to me. I understood that there is some connection between glorifying God and obeying God. What I failed to grasp is the link between all of this and "enjoying" God. If the chief end or purpose of my life was to enjoy God, then I was missing the purpose of my very existence. I dismissed this as antiquated religious language that had no relevance to my daily life. I certainly was not inclined to seek my joy in God.

I later understood my feelings when reading Luther's response to the question, "Do you love God?" Luther replied (prior to his conversion), "Love God? Sometimes I hate him!" This is a rare admission among men. Even Luther's candid reply was less than totally honest. Had he spoken the full truth, he would have said that he hated God all the time.

Moral Ability

As we noted earlier, much of the controversy between Pelagius and Augustine focused on the issue of the freedom of the human will. Pelagius believed the doctrine of original sin does violence to human freedom and responsibility. If Augustine assessed original sin correctly and we lack the ability not to sin (*non posse non peccare*), what does this do to free will? *The Westminster Confession of Faith* declares: "Man, by his fall into a state of sin, hath wholly lost all ability of will to any spiritual good accompanying salvation: so as, a natural man, being altogether averse from that good, and dead in sin, is not able, by his own strength, to convert himself, or to prepare himself thereunto."[4]

If ever the Reformed doctrine of total depravity has been crystallized into one brief statement, it is here. The moral inability of fallen man is the core concept of the doctrine of total depravity or radical corruption. If one embraces this aspect of the T in TULIP, the rest of the acrostic follows by a resistless logic. One cannot embrace the T and reject any of the other four letters with any degree of consistency.

Let us look carefully at this succinct summary of the Reformation concept of moral inability. First, the confession says that as a result of the fall, man "hath wholly lost all ability of will to any spiritual good accompanying salvation." Something has been not only lost, but *wholly* lost. It has been lost totally and in its entirety. It is not a partial loss or diminution of power or ability. It is a radical and complete loss. Yet this does not mean that the will's ability to choose has been lost completely. What has been lost is the ability to will "any good accompanying salvation."

We have already discussed the sinner's ability to perform works of civil virtue. These deeds conform outwardly to the law of God, but they are not motivated by a love for God. The moral ability lost in original sin is therefore not the ability to be outwardly "moral," but the ability to incline oneself to the things of God. In this spiritual dimension we are morally dead.

The confession declares that the natural man is "altogether averse from that good, and [he is] dead in sin." This summarizes the biblical description of fallen man. Paul describes the condition as follows:

> And you He made alive, who were dead in trespasses and sins, in which you once walked according to the course of this world, according to the prince of the power of the air, the spirit who now works in the sons of disobedience, among whom also we all once conducted ourselves in the lusts of our flesh, fulfilling the desires of the flesh and of the mind, and were by nature children of wrath, just as the others. But God, who is rich in mercy, because of His great love with which He loved us, even when we were dead in trespasses, made us alive together with Christ (by grace you have been saved). (Eph. 2:1–5)

In this passage Paul speaks of the Spirit's work in "quickening" us or regenerating us from our fallen condition. He uses the image of being "made alive." This is set in stark contrast to our former condition of being "dead" in trespasses and sins. The sinner is not biologically dead. Indeed the natural man is very much alive. Corpses do not sin. The death in view here is clearly spiritual death.

Paul speaks of the dead walking. They walk according to a certain course, which the apostle calls the course of this world. This path is diametrically opposed to the course or way of heaven. To take this path is to walk according to the prince of this world. Paul is obviously referring to Satan, so in our natural condition we are willing disciples of Satan. To be spiritually dead is to be diabolically alive.

In our former condition we willingly fulfilled the lusts of the flesh and the mind, behaving like creatures who are (because of original sin) by nature children of wrath. When Paul says we are children of wrath "by nature," he plunges a stake in the heart of Pelagianism. In this passage he provides a grim and graphic portrait of the natural man.

To be dead in sin is to be in a state of moral and spiritual bondage. By nature we are slaves to sin. This does not mean that the fall has destroyed or eradicated the human will. Fallen man still has all the faculties to make choices. We still have a mind and a will. The problem is not that we cannot make choices. Natural men make choices all the time. The problem is that, in our fallen condition, we make sinful choices. We make these choices freely. We sin precisely because we want to sin, and we are capable of choosing exactly what we want to choose.

Where then is the locus of our inability? The confession says that natural man is unable "to convert himself, or to prepare himself thereunto." If we still have a will, why are we unable to convert ourselves or even prepare ourselves for conversion? The simple answer is this: because we do not want to. We have no desire for the righteousness of God, and free choice, by definition, involves choosing what we desire.

Free Will

In one sense it is because our wills are free that we are in a state of moral inability. The thorny matter of free will is tied to the way our will functions. In his debate with Pelagius, Augustine insisted that fallen man retains a free will (*liberium arbitrium*). He insisted, however, that via original sin man loses the liberty (*libertas*) he enjoyed prior to the fall. On the surface it appears Augustine is playing word games. How can a person have a free will and not have liberty? This must be a distinction without a difference. The distinction, however, is both real and important. Man still has the ability to make choices, and in this sense he is free. But he lacks the capacity to exercise what Scripture calls "royal freedom," a liberty for spiritual obedience.

Calvin took a position similar to Augustine's: "This liberty is compatible with our being depraved, the servants of sin, able to do nothing but sin. In this way, then, man is said to have free will, not because he has a free choice of good and evil, but because he acts voluntarily, and not by compulsion. This is perfectly true: but why should so small a matter have been dignified with so proud a title? An admirable freedom! That man is not forced to be the servant of sin, while he is, however, *ethelodoulos* (a voluntary slave); his will being bound by the fetters of sin."[5]

Though Calvin affirmed that we are able to choose what we want, he regarded the term *free will* a bit grandiose for the matter. "Why should so small a matter," he asked, "have been dignified with so proud a title?" The title is indeed rooted in human pride. We like to think we have more moral power than we do. We think our will is utterly unaffected by original sin. This is the cardinal point of humanism. The humanistic and pagan view of free will is that the will acts from a posture of indifference. By *indifference* we mean that the will is inclined to neither good nor evil but exists in a state of moral neutrality. The mind of fallen man has no bias, no predisposition to evil. This view of free will is on a collision course with the biblical view of sin.

In his classic work *On the Freedom of the Will*, Jonathan Edwards defined the will as "the mind choosing." Edwards did not deny that there is a meaningful distinction between the mind and the will. They are distinct faculties. Although the mind and the will may be distinguished from each other, they may not be separated from each other. Moral actions involve rational choices. A mindless choice is not a moral choice. Plants may incline their roots toward water by a series of physical causes. But we do not judge this movement in terms of virtue or vice. These actions are involuntary. We also participate in involuntary actions. We do not decide to have our hearts pump blood through our circulatory system. This is an involuntary action. The brain may be involved in this process from a physiological vantage point, but not from the vantage point of conscious decision.

When Edwards spoke of the will as "the mind choosing," he meant that we make choices according to what we deem preferable in terms of the options before us. Edwards concluded that we always choose according to the inclination that is strongest at the moment. This is a crucial insight into the will. It means that every choice we make has an antecedent cause. Our choices are not "spontaneous," arising out of nothing. There is a reason for every choice we make. In a narrow sense every choice we make is *determined*.

To say that our choices are "determined" sounds very much like determinism. *Determinism*, however, means that our choices are controlled by external forces. This results in some form of coercion, which cancels out free choice. What Edwards had in mind is something different. Our choices are determined in the sense that they have a cause. This cause is the inclination of our will. This is *self*-determination, which is the very essence of free will. If I determine what I choose, this is not determinism, but it is a kind of determination. When we feel strongly about doing something, we may exclaim, "I am determined to do this." This refers to a strong desire or inclination of the will to move in a certain direction.

When Edwards says that we always choose according to our strongest inclination at the moment, he means not only that we *may* choose what we most want at the moment, but that we *must* choose it. Indeed, this is exactly how we make choices. Try to think of a choice you have made that was not in accord with your strongest inclination at the time. We sometimes get confused about this because we are assaulted with a wide variety of inclinations, and they change in intensity from time to time.

For example, after we have finished a heavy meal, it is easy to decide to go on a diet. With full stomachs we resolve to reduce our calorie intake. After a few hours, however, we become hungry again and the desire for food intensifies. If we reach the point that we want to eat some pie more than we want to lose weight, we choose the pie over the diet. All things being equal, we may want to shed excess weight. We have a real desire to be thin. But that desire or inclination runs up against our desire for culinary pleasures. The problem is that all things do not stay equal.

Another example may be seen in a Jack Benny skit. Benny was confronted by a robber who said to him, "Your money or your life."

Benny stood there mute, with a contemplative look on his face.

Growing impatient the robber said, "Well, which is it, your money or your life?"

"I'm thinking," Benny replied. "I'm thinking."

This story emphasizes that things are not always equal when we make choices. The robber reduces his victim's options to two: money or life. All things being equal, the victim has no desire to donate his money to the robber. Once death is threatened, however, the desire levels change. The victim has a greater desire to continue living than to keep his wallet, so he hands over his money. To be sure there is an element of coercion in this scenario, but the coercion is not absolute. It is extreme, but not final. The choice is still there to pay or die. A person may have such strong feelings against robbery that he prefers to die. He may cry, "Give me liberty or give me death," but he knows that even if he dies as a martyr to his cause, the robber will still take his money.

The point of this illustration is that we choose according to our strongest inclination at the moment. We must understand this as we seek to grow in our obedience to God. Every time I sin, I do so because at the moment I prefer the sin to obedience. I may have a real desire in my heart to be obedient, but this desire runs into conflict with my sinful desires. This is the dilemma expressed by the apostle Paul:

> For what I am doing, I do not understand. For what I will to do, that I do not practice; but what I hate, that I do. If, then, I do what I will not to do, I agree with the law that it is good. But now, it is no longer I who do it, but sin that dwells in me. For I know that in me (that is, in my flesh) nothing good dwells; for to will is present with me, but how to perform what is good I do not find. For the good that I will to do, I do not do; but the evil I will not to do, that I practice. (Rom. 7:15–19)

Paul is describing the conflict we face between rival inclinations, those toward the good and those toward evil. "The good that I will to do," he says, "I do not do." This does not undercut Edwards's view that we choose according to the strongest inclination. Christians do have a desire or will to do good. But we do not always do that good. At times we give in to our desire for evil. We do not do what we will to do because we do not will to do the good with sufficient intensity or strength. The whole process of sanctification involves this struggle. Paul likens it to warfare, a titanic battle between the spirit and the flesh.

The struggle between the spirit and the flesh is the struggle of the regenerate person. The unregenerate, natural man has no such struggle. He is in bondage to sin, acting according to the flesh, living according to the flesh, and choosing according to the flesh. He chooses according to the inclination that is dominant at the moment, and this inclination is never a desire to honor God out of a natural love for him. The desires of the unregenerate are wicked continuously. This is the bondage or spiritual death with which the doctrine of original sin is concerned.

Natural Ability

Edwards makes another important distinction, one between *natural ability* and *moral ability*. *Natural ability* is provided to a creature by the Creator. For example, birds have the natural ability to fly through the air without the aid of machines; human beings do not. Like fish, we have the natural ability to swim in the sea. Unlike fish, we cannot live in the sea without the aid of artificial equipment. God provides gills and fins for fish, feathers and wings for birds, but he has not endowed us with such equipment.

We human beings do have the natural ability, however, to make choices. We have been given the necessary natural equipment. We have a mind that can process information and understand the obligations imposed by the law of God. We have a will that enables us to choose to do what we want to do. Prior to the fall we also had a good inclination, enabling us to choose the good. It is precisely this inclination to the good that was lost in the fall. Original sin does not destroy our humanity or our ability to make choices. The natural ability or faculty remains intact. What was lost is the good inclination or righteous desire for obedience. The unregenerate person is not inclined to obey God. He has no love for God that stirs his will to choose God. He could choose the things of God *if he wanted them*, but he does not want them. Our wills are such that we cannot freely choose what we have no desire to choose. The fundamental loss of a desire for God is the heart of original sin.

The lack of desire for the things of God renders us morally unable to choose the good. This is what Edwards means when he distinguishes between natural ability and moral ability. Fallen man has the natural ability to choose God (the necessary faculties of choice), but he lacks the moral ability to do so. The ability to make righteous moral choices requires righteous desires and inclinations. Without a righteous inclination to the good, no one can choose the good. Our choices follow our inclinations. For man to be able to choose the things of God, he must first be inclined to choose them. Since the flesh makes no provision for the things of God, grace is required for us to be able to choose them. The unregenerate person must be regenerated before he has any desire for God. The spiritually dead must first be made alive ("quickened") by the Holy Spirit before they have any desire for God.

> [Jesus said,] "It is the Spirit who gives life; the flesh profits nothing. The words that I speak to you are spirit, and they are life. But there are some of you who do not believe." For Jesus knew from the beginning who they were who did not believe, and who would betray Him. And He said, "Therefore I have said to you that no one can come to Me unless it has been granted to him by My Father." From that time many of His disciples went back and walked with Him no more. Then Jesus said to the twelve, "Do you also want to go away?" Then Simon Peter answered Him, "Lord, to whom shall we go? You have the words of eternal life." (John 6:63–68)

On this occasion Jesus spoke about the moral impotence of the flesh. He taught his disciples that the flesh "profits nothing." Perhaps his most startling comment is this: "No one can come to Me unless it has been granted to him by My Father." This statement is a universal negative proposition. It states a universal inability. The word *can* does not describe permission, but power or ability. To say no one can do something is to say they are unable to do it. The stark truth expressed by Jesus is that no person has the ability to come to Christ on his or her own. For a person to be able to come to Christ, it must first be granted or "given" to that person to come to Christ. God must do something for us to overcome our moral inability to come to Christ. We cannot embrace Christ in the flesh. Without the aid of the Holy Spirit, we cannot come to Christ.

Jesus's statement about our natural inability to come to him is a strong and radical one. It is as strong as the position taken by Augustine, Calvin, Luther, and Edwards. Indeed these theologians were heavily influenced by these words of Christ. His audience reacted strongly to Jesus's teaching: many of his followers left him. I suppose they left to join the ranks of the Pelagians of that day. Baptist theologian Roger Nicole once remarked, "We are all by nature Pelagians." We tend to think in Pelagian categories and find it difficult to escape them. Even conversion to Christ does not instantly cure us of this tendency. Pelagianism remains alive and well in the evangelical house.

Because of our depravity and the effects of original sin, we find liberation only by the grace of God. The *Westminster Confession* says this:

When God converts a sinner, and translates him into the state of grace, He freeth him from his natural bondage under sin; and, by His grace alone, enables him freely to will and to do that which is spiritually good; yet so, as that by reason of his remaining corruption, he doth not perfectly, nor only, will that which is good, but doth also will that which is evil.

The will of man is made perfectly and immutably free to do good alone in the state of glory only.[6]

The confession understands that a person who is inclined in only one direction, whether to the good or to the evil, is still free in a certain sense. This freedom is real. For example, God is totally free, yet he is morally unable to sin. This inability is rooted in his character, his internal righteousness by which he never desires or is inclined to sin. He is free, but free only for goodness. This lack of desire for evil does not diminish God's freedom; it enhances it.

Likewise, in our glorified state in heaven we will be unable to sin because all desire for sin and all remnants of original sin will be removed from us. We will still be free to choose what we want, but we will choose only the good because this is the only thing we will desire. This is the freedom Augustine referred to as liberty in the ultimate degree.

7

GOD'S SOVEREIGN
CHOICE

When someone mentions the term *Calvinism*, the customary response is, "Oh, you mean the doctrine of predestination?" This identification of Calvinism with predestination is as strange as it is real and widespread.

Calvinism certainly does hold firmly to the biblical doctrine of predestination. The Reformed view of the doctrine is central to historic Calvinism. Virtually nothing in John Calvin's view of predestination, however, was not first in Martin Luther, and before Luther in Augustine (and arguably in Thomas Aquinas). Luther wrote more about the subject than did Calvin. Calvin's treatment of predestination in his famous *Institutes of the Christian Religion* is sparse in comparison to other doctrines.

Almost every church has developed some form of the doctrine of predestination simply because the Bible teaches predestination. Predestination is a biblical word and a biblical concept. If one seeks to develop a theology that is biblical, one cannot avoid the doctrine of predestination. The term *predestination* or *predestined* is used liberally by the apostle Paul:

> Blessed be the God and Father of our Lord Jesus Christ, who has blessed us with every spiritual blessing in the heavenly places in Christ, just as He chose us in Him before the foundation of the world, that we should be holy and without blame before Him in love, having predestined us to adoption as sons by Jesus Christ to Himself, according to the good pleasure of His will, to the praise of the glory of His grace, by which He has made us accepted in the Beloved. . . . [He] made known to us the mystery of His will, according to His good pleasure which He purposed in Himself, that in the dispensation of the fullness of the times He might gather together in one all things in Christ, both which are in heaven and which are on earth—in Him. . . . [In Him] also we have obtained an inheritance, being predestined according to the purpose of Him who works all things according to the counsel of His will, that we who first trusted in Christ should be to the praise of His glory. (Eph. 1:3–12)

Paul speaks of believers being predestined according to the counsel of God's will. The question then is not, Does the Bible teach predestination? The question is, What exactly does the biblical concept of predestination mean? In its most basic sense predestination has to do with the question of destiny. A destiny or a destination is a point toward which we are moving but have not yet reached. When we book airline tickets, we do not book them to nowhere. We have a destination in mind, a place we are trying to reach.

When we add the prefix *pre* to *destination*, we speak of something that takes place prior to or before the destination. The *pre* of *predestination* relates to the question of time. In biblical categories predestination clearly takes place, not only before we believe in Christ, and not only before we were even born, but from all eternity, before the universe was ever created.

The agent of predestination is God. In his sovereignty he predestinates. Human beings are the object of his predestination. In short, predestination refers to God's sovereign plan for human beings, decreed by him in eternity. We must add, however, that the concept of predestination includes more than the future destiny of humans. It also includes whatever comes to pass in time and space. Often the term *election* is used as a synonym for *predestination*. Technically this is incorrect. The term *election* refers specifically to one aspect of divine predestination: God's choosing of certain individuals to be saved. The term *election* has a positive connotation, referring to a benevolent predestination that results in the salvation of those who are elect. *Election* also has a negative side, called "reprobation," which involves the predestination of those who are not elect.

Table 7.1
The Tulip's Second Petal

1	**T**otal depravity	Humanity's radical corruption
2	**Unconditional election**	God's sovereign choice
3	**L**imited atonement	Christ's purposeful atonement
4	**I**rresistible grace	The Spirit's effective call
5	**P**erseverance of the saints	God's preservation of the saints

In summary we may define *predestination* broadly as follows: From all eternity God decided to save some members of the human race and to let the rest of the human race perish. God made a choice—he chose some individuals to be saved unto everlasting blessedness in heaven, and he chose others to pass over, allowing them to suffer the consequences of their sins, eternal punishment in hell.

Conditional or Unconditional?

Do our individual lives have any bearing on God's decision? This is a difficult issue and one that must be treated with great care. Even though God makes his choice before we are born, he still knows everything about us and our lives before we live them. Does he take that prior knowledge of us into account when he makes his decision regarding election? How we answer this question reveals whether our view of predestination is Reformed or not Reformed. The issue is this: On what does God base his decision to elect some and not others?

In the acrostic TULIP the U refers to "unconditional election." The word *unconditional* distinguishes the Reformed doctrine of predestination from that of other theologies. During the Civil War Ulysses S. Grant was nicknamed "Unconditional Surrender" Grant, retaining his initials U. S. Unconditional surrender in warfare is a surrender that excludes negotiations. There is no room for "I'll do this if you do that." The surrender is total and complete. The defeated foe surrenders all, while the victor surrenders nothing. This type of surrender, observed aboard the battleship USS Missouri, brought an end to

World War II. The term *unconditional* simply means "with no conditions attached, either foreseen or otherwise."

Many non-Reformed churches teach that election is conditional: God elects certain people to salvation, but only if they meet certain conditions. Not that God waits for these people to meet these conditions before he chooses them. Conditional election is usually based on God's foreknowledge of human actions and responses. This is often called the *prescient view* of election or predestination. The term *prescience* or *pre-science* simply refers to foreknowledge. The idea is that from all eternity God looks down the tunnel of time and knows in advance who will respond to the gospel positively and who will not. He knows in advance who will exercise faith and who will not. On the basis of this prior knowledge, God chooses some. He elects them because he knows they will have faith. He knows who will meet the conditions for election and on that basis elects them.

The favorite proof text for the prescient view of election is in Romans: "For whom He foreknew, He also predestined to be conformed to the image of His Son, that He might be the firstborn among many brethren. Moreover whom He predestined, these He also called; whom He called, these He also justified; and whom He justified, these He also glorified" (Rom. 8:29–30).

We notice in this text that God's foreknowledge precedes his predestination. Those who advocate the prescient view assume that, since foreknowledge precedes predestination, foreknowledge must be the basis of predestination. Paul does not say this. He simply says that God predestined those whom he foreknew. Who else could he possibly predestine? Before God can choose anyone for anything, he must have them in mind as objects of his choice. That Paul links predestination with foreknowledge says nothing about whether this foreknowledge includes the person's meeting some condition for election.

In actuality Romans 8:29–30 militates against the prescient view of election. Paul begins with foreknowledge and then progresses through the "golden chain" of salvation via predestination, calling, justification, and glorification. The crucial question here is the relationship between calling and justification. The chain says that those whom God foreknew he also predestined. The text is elliptical: it does not include the term *all* but it tacitly implies the word (most translations of the Bible add it). The sense of the text is that all whom God foreknows (in whatever sense he foreknows them) he predestines. And all whom he predestines he calls. And all whom he calls he justifies. And all whom he justifies he glorifies. The chain is: foreknowledge–predestination–calling–justification–glorification.

It is significant that all who are called are also justified. What does Paul mean here by "calling"? In theology we distinguish between two kinds of divine calling: the *external* and the *internal* call.

We see the external call of God in the preaching of the gospel. Everyone who hears the gospel preached is called or summoned to Christ. But not everyone responds positively to this outward call. Some ignore it and others flatly reject it. Sometimes the gospel falls on deaf ears. Scripture is clear that not everyone who hears the gospel outwardly is automatically justified. Justification is not by hearing the call but by believing the call. So, at least in some sense, there are some (indeed many) who are called but who are not chosen. Many hear that external call of the gospel who are never justified. Yet in the golden chain Paul says that those who are called by God are also justified by him. Unless one is a universalist, one cannot conclude that this refers simply to the outward call of the gospel.

Theology also speaks of the inward call of God, which is not given to everyone. Reformed theology calls it *effectual calling* (which will be discussed more fully in chapter 9). All who get this call are included in those who are justified. Again this assumes the text implies that *all* who are called are justified. The text does not say that explicitly. It is possible to interpret the text to mean that *some* who are called are justified. But if the term *some* is implied here at this point in the chain, it must be implied throughout the chain. In this case the text would say that some whom God foreknew he predestined, some whom he predestined he called, some whom he called he justified, and some whom he justified he glorified. This makes nonsense out of Paul's words. The implication of *all* is not vague and uncertain. It is clearly implied by the wording of the text.

The Order of Salvation

We are dealing here with the order of salvation (*ordo salutis*). We note that predestination precedes calling. If calling preceded predestination, a case could be made for the prescient view. Then it could be assumed that predestination is based on calling rather than calling on predestination (although the difference between the external call and the internal call would still be problematic).

Reformed theology understands the golden chain to mean that God predestines some people to receive a divine call that others do not receive. Only the predestined, or the elect, receive this call, and only those who receive this call are justified. A process of selection is clearly involved here. Not everyone is predestined to receive this call, the consequence of which is justification. Likewise it is clear that only those who are predestined are justified. Since justification is by faith, we understand that only the predestined will ever have faith. The prescient view holds that we are elected because we will have faith. The Reformed view holds that we are elected *unto* faith and justification. Faith is a necessary condition for salvation, but not for election. The prescient view makes faith a condition of election; Reformed theology sees faith as the result of election. This is the fundamental difference between conditional election and unconditional election, between all forms of semi-Pelagianism and Augustinianism, between Arminianism and Calvinism.

Reformed theologians understand the golden chain as follows: From all eternity God foreknew his elect. He had an idea of their identity in his mind before he created them. He foreknew them not only in the sense of having a prior idea of their personal identities, but also in the sense of foreloving them. When the Bible speaks of "knowing," it often distinguishes between a simple mental awareness of a person and a deep intimate love of a person. The Reformed view teaches that all whom God has foreknown, he has also predestined to be inwardly called, justified, and glorified. God sovereignly brings to pass the salvation of his elect and only of his elect.

The *Westminster Confession* declares:

Fig. 7.1

The Golden Chain of Salvation

By the decree of God, for the manifestation of His glory, some men and angels are predestined unto everlasting life; and others foreordained to everlasting death.

These angels and men, thus predestined, and foreordained, are particularly and unchangeably designed, and their number so certain and definite, that it cannot be either increased or diminished.

Those of mankind that are predestined unto life, God, before the foundation of the world was laid, according to His eternal and immutable purpose, and the secret counsel and good pleasure of His will, hath chosen, in Christ, unto everlasting glory, out of His mere free grace and love, without any foresight of faith, or good works, or perseverance in either of them, or any other thing in the creature, as conditions, or causes moving Him thereunto: and all to the praise of His glorious grace.[1]

The confession spells out what is meant by unconditional election. The grounds of our election are not something foreseen by God in us but rather the good pleasure of his sovereign will. Here the sovereignty of God refers not only to his power and authority but also to his grace. This echoes what Paul emphatically declares in Romans:

> When Rebecca also had conceived by one man, even by our father Isaac (for the children not yet being born, nor having done any good or evil, that the purpose of God according to election might stand, not of works but of Him who calls), it was said to her, "The older shall serve the younger." As it is written, "Jacob I have loved, but Esau I have hated."
>
> What shall we say then? Is there unrighteousness with God? Certainly not! For He says to Moses, "I will have mercy on whomever I will have mercy, and I will have compassion on whomever I will have compassion." So then it is not of him who wills, nor of him who runs, but of God who shows mercy. (Rom. 9:10–16)

Paul reminds the Romans of what God had declared to Moses: "I will have mercy on whomever I will have mercy, and I will have compassion on whomever I will have compassion." The principle is that of the sovereignty of God's mercy and grace. By definition grace is not something God is required to have. It is his sovereign prerogative to grant or withhold it. God does not owe grace to anyone. Grace that is owed is not grace. Justice imposes obligation, but grace, in its essence, is voluntary and free.

The ground on which God chooses the objects of his mercy is solely the good pleasure of his will. Paul makes this clear: "Blessed be the God and Father of our Lord Jesus Christ, who has blessed us with every spiritual blessing in the heavenly places in Christ, just as He chose us in Him before the foundation of the world, that we should be holy and without blame before Him in love, having predestined us to adoption as sons by Jesus Christ to Himself, according to the good pleasure of His will . . ." (Eph. 1:3–5).

That God chooses according to the good pleasure of his will does not mean that his choices are capricious or arbitrary. An arbitrary choice is one made for no reason at all. Though Reformed theology insists that God's election is based on nothing foreseen in the individuals' lives, this does not mean that he makes the choice for no reason at all. It simply means that the reason is not something God finds in us. In his inscrutable, mysterious will, God chooses for reasons known only to himself. He chooses according to his own pleasure, which is his divine right. His pleasure is described as his *good* pleasure. If something pleases God, it must be good. There is no evil pleasure in God.

In all forms of semi-Pelagianism, in the final analysis, the grounds of God's election rest inevitably in the actions of men. Here is where we see the pervasive influence of Pelagianism on the modern church.

Paul states emphatically that the grounds of God's election of Jacob over Esau did not lie in the actions of either brother. The first thing we note about the apostle's statement is that it refers to individuals. Some have argued that Paul is referring instead to nations or groups and that election does not apply to individuals. Apart from the fact that nations are made up of individuals, the salient point is that Paul explains election by citing as examples of God's sovereign election two distinct, historical individuals. These individuals were as close as two people can be. They were not only brothers of one family, they were twin brothers.

Paul says that God's decree of election transpired before the children were born or had done anything good or evil. Why does the apostle say this? What is the didactic or literary purpose of saying that the twins were not yet born or had not yet done anything good or evil? The prescient view of conditional election agrees that God's election occurred before the twins were born and before they had done anything good or evil. But that is to labor the obvious.

The prescient view then states that the decree was nevertheless based on the twins' actions and decisions in the future. The apostle nowhere says that. If Paul had intended to teach the prescient view, he could have said precisely that. But we are dealing here with more than an argument from silence. Paul makes it clear that it was not the actions of Jacob or Esau that determined God's sovereign choice of Jacob over Esau: "It is not of him who wills, nor of him who runs, but of God who shows mercy."

In Arminianism the decisive factor in election is the willing of the believer. How could the apostle have made it clearer that this is not the case than by saying that "it is not of [by] him who wills"? Arminians and semi-Pelagians ultimately rest their view of election on the one who wills and not on the sovereign grace of God. The prescient view of election is not so much an explanation of the biblical doctrine of election as a flat denial of this biblical doctrine.

Election and God's Righteousness

In Romans Paul asks a rhetorical question: "What shall we say then? Is there unrighteousness with[in] God?" Again we ask why Paul asked this question. He was a teacher par excellence. He anticipated objections that might be raised by his teaching, and he dealt with them up front. What objection does he have in view when he raises the question of unrighteousness in God?

First we consider the prescient view of election. What objections raised against it include the charge that there is unrighteousness in God? None. The conditional view of election is designed to protect two borders: on one side a particular view of human freedom, and on the other side a particular view of God. They seek to protect God from the charge that he is unfair, arbitrary, or unjust, choosing some persons for salvation without a view to their own choices. In short, opposition to Arminian or semi-Pelagian views of election does not include the accusation that it places in doubt the righteousness of God. If Paul were espousing the prescient view, we would hardly expect him to anticipate an objection of this sort.

The objection Paul does anticipate is one that Calvinists hear constantly: the Calvinist doctrine of election casts a shadow over God's righteousness. The complaint is loud and frequent that unconditional election involves God in a kind of unrighteousness. My guess is that Paul anticipated the very objection that Calvinists hear because he taught the same doctrine of election that Calvinists teach. When our doctrine of election is assailed, I take comfort that we are in good company, that of Paul himself, when we must bear the cavils of those who oppose unconditional election.

The idea that there may be unrighteousness in God is related to God's choice of some for salvation while passing over others. It does not seem fair or "right" for God to bestow his grace on some but not on others. If the decision to bless Jacob over Esau was made before either was born or had done anything good or evil, and if the choice was not with a view to their future actions or responses, then the obvious question is, Why did one receive the blessing and not the other? Paul answers by appealing to God's words to Moses: "I will have mercy on whomever I will have mercy." It is God's prerogative to dispense his grace however he sees fit. He owed neither Jacob nor Esau any measure of grace. Had he chosen neither, he would have violated no precept of justice or righteousness.

It still seems that if God gives grace to one person, in the interest of fairness he "ought" to give grace equally to another. It is precisely this "oughtness" that is foreign to the biblical concept of grace. Among the mass of fallen humanity, all guilty of sin before God and exposed to his justice, no one has any claim or entitlement to God's mercy. If God chooses to grant mercy to some of that group, this does not require that he give it to all.

God certainly has the power and authority to grant his saving grace to all mankind. Clearly he has not elected to do this. All men are not saved despite the fact that God has the power and right to save them all if that is his good pleasure. It is also clear that all are not lost. God could have chosen not to save anyone. He has the power and authority to execute his righteous justice by saving nobody. In reality he elects to save some, but not all. Those who are saved are beneficiaries of his sovereign grace and mercy. Those who are not saved are not victims of his cruelty or injustice; they are recipients of justice. No one receives punishment at the hands of God that they do not deserve. Some receive grace at his hands that they do not deserve. Because he is pleased to grant mercy to one does not mean that the rest "deserve" the same. If mercy is deserved, it is not really mercy, but justice.

Biblical history makes it clear that though God is never unjust to anyone, he does not treat all people equally or the same. For example, God in his grace called Abraham out of his paganism in Ur of the Chaldees and made a gracious covenant with him that he did not make with other pagans. God revealed himself to Moses in a manner he did not grant to Pharaoh. God gave Saul of Tarsus a blessed revelation of the majesty of Christ that he did not give to Pilate or Caiaphas. Because God was so gracious to Paul when he was a violent persecutor of Christians, was God therefore obliged to give the same revelatory advantage to Pilate?

Or was there a special virtuous quality in Saul that inclined God to choose him above Pilate? We could leap over the centuries to our own day with a similar question. We believers must ask ourselves why we have come to faith while many of our friends have not. Did we exercise faith in Christ because we are more intelligent than they are? If so, where did this intelligence come from? Is it something we earned or deserved? Or was our intelligence itself a gift from our Creator? Did we respond to the gospel positively because we are better or more virtuous than our friends?

We all know the answers to these questions. I cannot adequately explain why I came to faith in Christ and some of my friends did not. I can only look to the glory of God's grace toward me, a grace I did not deserve then and do not deserve now. Here the rubber meets the road, and we discover if we are harboring a secret pride, believing that we deserve salvation more than others. Here is a gross insult to God's grace and a monument to our arrogance. It is a reversion to the worst form of legalism, by which we ultimately put our trust in our own work.

Election and Moral Inability

Those who favor a conditional view of election or some sort of prescience as the basis of election face a serious difficulty. They must assume that fallen persons are morally capable of responding positively to the gospel. This assumption is semi-Pelagian because it presupposes that original sin weakens the will but does not render it morally unable to incline itself to the things of God. Original sin notwithstanding, there remains some spontaneous power in the flesh that can incline itself to spiritual things. We said earlier that if one agrees with the doctrine of total depravity, the T in TULIP, then the U of unconditional election follows necessarily. If one is incapable of meeting the conditions, then election must be unconditional. If the Reformation view of original sin is correct, then God would see no fallen creature choose Christ in the future. God would know from all eternity that, left to themselves, fallen creatures will not choose Christ.

As we have seen, the Gospel of John reports that Christ addressed this matter:

> [Jesus said,] "But there are some of you who do not believe." For Jesus knew from the beginning who they were who did not believe, and who would betray Him. And He said, "Therefore I have said to you that no one can come to Me unless it has been granted to him by My Father." From that time many of His disciples went back and walked with Him no more. Then Jesus said to the twelve, "Do you also want to go away?" Then Simon Peter answered Him, "Lord, to whom shall we go? You have the words of eternal life." (John 6:64–68)

Jesus says that no one can come to him without a grant from the Father. John relates this to the comment that Jesus knew from the beginning those who did not believe and would betray him. Again the reaction to the teaching of Jesus is telling: many of his disciples deserted him. Why were they offended by Jesus's words? If the words are given an Arminian cast, we see no reason for the offense. Only if we understand Jesus's words to teach moral inability and an utter dependence on God's grace does offense become intelligible. The doctrine of moral inability has offended many, and many have rejected Reformed theology precisely because of it.

Also interesting is Peter's reaction to Jesus's words. Jesus asked Peter, "Do you also want to go away?"

"Lord, to whom shall we go?" Peter responds. "You have the words of eternal life."

This reply suggests that Peter was less than enamored with Jesus's teaching. He may have been saying: "I don't like this doctrine any more than those who walked away, but where else can we go? You are the teacher we trust and follow. You have the words of eternal life, so we'll stick with you even if you teach some hard things."

Earlier in John's Gospel, Jesus says something similar regarding moral inability: "Do not murmur among yourselves. No one can come to Me unless the Father who sent Me draws him; and I will raise him up at the last day" (John 6:43–44). The key word in this statement is *draw*. What is meant by this drawing? I have often heard it explained that, for a person to come to Christ, God the Holy Spirit must first woo or entice them to come. We have the ability, however, to resist this wooing and refuse the enticement.

Though this wooing is a necessary condition for coming to Christ, it is not a sufficient condition. It is necessary but not compelling. We cannot come to Christ without being wooed, but the wooing does not guarantee that we will come to Christ.

I am persuaded that this explanation is incorrect. It does violence to the text of Scripture, particularly to the biblical meaning of the word *draw*. The Greek word used is *elkō*. Gerhard Kittel's *Theological Dictionary of the New Testament* defines *elkō* to mean "to compel by irresistible superiority." Linguistically and lexicographically the word means simply "to compel."[2]

"Compel" is much more forceful than "woo." To see the force of this verb, let us examine two other passages in the New Testament where *elkō* is used. The first passage is in James 2:6: "But you have dishonored the poor man. Do not the rich oppress you and drag [*elkō*] you into the courts?" If we substitute the word *woo* here, the text would read: "Do not the rich oppress you and woo you into the courts?"

The second passage is Acts 16:19: "But when her masters saw that their hope of profit was gone, they seized Paul and Silas and dragged [*elkō*] them into the marketplace to the authorities." It would be ludicrous to say Paul and Silas were "wooed" to the authorities. Once forcibly seized, they could not be enticed or wooed. The text clearly indicates they were *compelled* to come before the authorities.

I was once asked to participate in a formal debate on the subject of election at an Arminian seminary. My opponent was the head of the New Testament department. At a crucial point in the debate, we focused our attention on the Father's "drawing" people to Christ. My opponent appealed to John 6:44 to make his case that God "draws" men to Christ but never compels them to come. He insisted that the divine influence on fallen man is restricted to drawing, which he interpreted to mean "wooing."

At that point I referred him to Kittel and to the other passages in the New Testament that translate the word *elkō* with the word *drag*. The professor was ready for me. He cited an instance in Greek drama where the same word is used to describe the action of drawing water from a well. He looked at me and said, "Well, Professor Sproul, does one drag water from a well?" Instantly the audience erupted in laughter at this use of the Greek word.

When the laughter subsided, I replied: "No, sir, I have to admit that we do not drag water from a well. But how do we get water from a well? Do we woo it? Do we stand at the top of the well and cry, 'Here, water, water, water'?"

It is as necessary for God to turn us to Christ as it is for us to pull up the bucket to drink water from the well. The water will simply not come out on its own, no matter how hard we plead.

The question of drawing or wooing must be examined further. When the Arminian speaks of the Spirit's wooing, does he believe the Spirit's action is external to the person or internal? Is the drawing simply the outward pull or tug of the preaching of the Word? Or does the Holy Spirit somehow penetrate to the soul and then do his work of enticement? Is it an attempt at inner persuasion? If so, the Spirit's action is still external to the soul because he does nothing that is actually compelling to the soul.

Other difficult questions are faced by Arminians at this point. Two important issues are these: (1) Does God woo or draw all men equally? (2) Why do some people respond favorably to the Holy Spirit's wooing?

As for the first question, if God does not woo all people equally, then all the objections to the Reformed view of unconditional election must be raised here as well. Does God not draw all men equally because some have greater power to respond than others? The Arminian may answer that God draws only those whom he knows will respond favorably. If so, then God does not even woo those who never come to faith. Few if any Arminians are willing to say that.

The second question is this: Why do some respond favorably to the Holy Spirit rather than refuse his wooing? If we say the answer lies in the intensity of the wooing (namely, that the Spirit entices some more strongly than others), then we are back to the problem of sovereign selection. If we say instead that some respond favorably to the wooing because of something found in them, then we root our salvation ultimately in a human work. Does one respond to the wooing positively due to greater intelligence or greater virtue? If so, then we have something to boast about.

When I pose this question to my Arminian friends, they readily see the dilemma and seek to avoid it by saying: "Certainly it is not a matter of intelligence or of any inherent superior virtue in those who respond positively. They respond this way because they see their need for Christ more clearly." With this reply they dig themselves deeper into the pit. The answer only postpones the problem one step.

Why do some people see their need for Christ more clearly than do others? Have they received greater illumination from the Holy Spirit? Are they more intelligent? Are they less prejudiced toward Christ and more open to his call, which is itself a virtue? No matter how one delays it, sooner or later we must face the question of greater or lesser inherent virtue.

Following Paul's lead in Ephesians, Reformed theology teaches that faith itself is a gift given to the elect. God himself creates the faith in the believer's heart. God fulfills the necessary condition for salvation, and he does so without condition. Again we look to Paul's words: "For by grace you have been saved through faith, and that not of yourselves; it is the gift of God, not of works, lest anyone should boast. For we are His workmanship, created in Christ Jesus for good works, which God prepared beforehand that we should walk in them" (Eph. 2:8–10).

Considerable debate has ensued regarding the meaning of the first sentence. What is the antecedent for the word *that*: *grace*, *saved*, or *faith*? The rules of Greek syntax and grammar demand that the antecedent of *that* be the word *faith*. Paul is declaring what every Reformed person affirms, that faith is a gift from God. Faith is not something we conjure up by our own effort, or the result of the willing of the flesh. Faith is a result of the Spirit's sovereign work of regeneration. It is no accident that this statement concludes a passage that begins with Paul's declaration that we have been "quickened" or "made alive" while we were in a state of spiritual death.

Double Predestination?

Any time the subject of predestination or election arises, the question quickly follows, "Is predestination single or double?" Usually lurking behind this question is a thinly veiled query regarding infra- or supralapsarianism. Since that issue is somewhat arcane, we will not treat it here. The deeper issue is how reprobation relates to election. Reprobation is the flip side of election, the dark side of the matter that raises many concerns. It is the doctrine of reprobation that has prompted the label of "horrible decree." It is one thing to speak of God's gracious predestination to election, but quite another to speak of God's decreeing from all eternity that certain unfortunate people are destined for damnation.

Some advocates of predestination argue for *single* predestination. They maintain that, though some are predestined to election, no one is predestined to damnation or reprobation. God chooses some whom he will definitely save, but he leaves open the opportunity for salvation for the rest. God makes sure that some people are saved by providing special help, but the rest of mankind still has an opportunity to be saved. They can somehow *become* elect by responding positively to the gospel.

This view is based more on sentiment than on logic or exegesis. It is manifestly obvious that if some people are elect and some are not elect, then predestination has two sides to it. It is not enough to speak of Jacob; we must also consider Esau. Unless predestination is universal, either to universal election or universal reprobation, it must be double in some sense.

Given that the Bible teaches both election and particularism, we cannot avoid the subject of double predestination.

The question then is not *if* predestination is double, but *how* it is double. There are different views of double predestination. One of them is so frightening that many shun altogether the use of the term *double predestination*. This scary view is called *equal ultimacy*, and it is based on a symmetrical view of predestination. It sees a symmetry between the work of God in election and his work in reprobation. It seeks an exact balance between the two. Just as God intervenes in the lives of the elect to create faith in their hearts, so he similarly intervenes in the hearts of the reprobate to work unbelief. The latter is inferred from biblical passages that speak of God's hardening people's hearts.

Classical Reformed theology rejects the doctrine of equal ultimacy. Though some have labeled this doctrine "hyper-Calvinism," I prefer to call it "sub-Calvinism," or even more precisely, "anti-Calvinism." Though Calvinism certainly holds to a kind of double predestination, it does not embrace equal ultimacy. The Reformed view makes a crucial distinction between God's *positive* and *negative* decrees. God positively decrees the election of some, and he negatively decrees the reprobation of others. The difference between positive and negative does not refer to the outcome (though the outcome indeed is either positive or negative), but to the manner by which God brings his decrees to pass in history.

The positive side refers to God's active intervention in the lives of the elect to work faith in their hearts. The negative refers, not to God's working unbelief in the hearts of the reprobate, but simply to his passing them by and withholding his regenerating grace from them.

Calvin comments on this: "Now, if we are not really ashamed of the Gospel, we must of necessity acknowledge what is therein openly declared: that God by His eternal goodwill (for which there was no other cause than His own purpose), appointed those whom He pleased unto salvation, rejecting all the rest; and that those whom He blessed with this free adoption to be His sons He illumines by His Holy Spirit, that they may receive the life which is offered to them in Christ; while others, continuing of their own will in unbelief, are left destitute of the light of faith, in total darkness."[3]

For Calvin and other Reformers God passes over the reprobate, leaving them to their own devices. He does not coerce them to sin or create fresh evil in their hearts. He leaves them to themselves, to their own choices and desires, and they always choose to reject the gospel.

I once heard the president of a Presbyterian seminary respond to a question about predestination by saying, "I don't believe in predestination because I do not believe God brings some people kicking and screaming, against their wills, into his kingdom, while at the same time he refuses access to those who earnestly desire to be there." This response surprised me, not only because the president's public disavowal of predestination blatantly violated his ordination vows in the Presbyterian church, but also because it revealed a radical misunderstanding of a doctrine with which he should have been quite familiar.

Reformed theology does not teach that God brings the elect "kicking and screaming, against their wills," into his kingdom. It teaches that God so works in the hearts of the elect as to make them willing and pleased to come to Christ. They come to Christ because they want to. They want to because God has created in their hearts a desire for Christ. Likewise the reprobate do not want to embrace Christ earnestly. They have no desire for Christ whatever and are fleeing from him.

Table 7.2
Predestination of the Elect (PE) and of the Reprobate (PR)

Orthodox Calvinism	Hyper-Calvinism
PE is positive; PR is **negative**.	PE is positive; PR is **positive**.
PE and PR are **asymmetrical**.	PE and PR are **symmetrical**.
The ultimacy of PE and the ultimacy of PR are **unequal**.	The ultimacy of PE and the ultimacy of PR are **equal**.
PR: God **passes over** the reprobate.	PR: God **works unbelief** in the reprobate's heart.

Table 7.2 demonstrates the difference between orthodox Calvinism and what is called hyper-Calvinism. In this table we see Calvinism's positive-negative schema, in which God actively works in the lives and hearts of the elect, while he passes over the reprobate or leaves him in his natural condition. It is important to remember that in his decree of election, God considers the mass of mankind in their fallen sinful condition. He chooses to redeem some people from this condition and to leave the rest in that condition. He intervenes in the lives of the elect, while he does not intervene in the lives of the reprobate. One group receives mercy and the other receives justice.

The concept of *justice* incorporates all that is just. The concept of *non-justice* includes everything outside the concept of justice: *injustice*, which violates justice and is evil; and *mercy*, which does not violate justice and is not evil. God gives his mercy (non-justice) to some and leaves the rest to his justice. No one is treated with injustice. No one can charge that there is unrighteousness in God.

When Paul speaks of God's having loved Jacob and hated Esau (Rom. 9:13), this divine "hatred" must not be equated with human hatred. It is a holy hatred (see Ps. 139:22). Divine hatred is never malicious. It withholds favor. God is "for" his elect in a special way, displaying his love for them. He turns his face away from those wicked people who are not the objects of his special grace. Those whom he loves with his "love of complacency" receive his mercy. Those whom he "hates" receive his justice. No one is treated in an unjust manner.

We conclude that the election of which the Bible speaks is unconditional. No foreseen actions of the elect cause them to be elect or provide the grounds of their election. The conditions for salvation or justification are indeed met by the believer, but they are met because God provides these conditions for them by his sovereign grace. Calvin summarized it this way:

> Many controvert all the positions which we have laid down, especially the gratuitous election of believers, which however cannot be overthrown. For they commonly imagine that God distinguishes between men according to the merits which he foresees that each individual is to have, giving the adoption of sons to those whom he foreknows will not be unworthy of his grace, and dooming those to destruction whose dispositions he perceives will be prone to mischief and wickedness. Thus by interposing foreknowledge as a veil, they not only obscure election, but pretend to give it a different origin.[4]

8

CHRIST'S PURPOSEFUL
ATONEMENT

The primary axiom of all Reformed theology is this: "Salvation is of the Lord." Salvation is a divine work. It is designed and ordained by the Father, accomplished by the Son, and applied by the Holy Spirit. All three persons of the Trinity are in eternal agreement on the plan of redemption and its execution.

On the distinction between Reformed and Arminian theology, J. I. Packer has written:

> The difference between them is not primarily one of emphasis, but of content. One proclaims a God who saves; the other speaks of a God who enables man to save himself. One view presents the three great acts of the Holy Trinity for the recovering of lost mankind—election by the Father, redemption by the Son, calling by the Spirit—as directed towards the same persons, and as securing their salvation

infallibly. The other view gives each act a different reference (the objects of redemption being all mankind, of calling, those who hear the gospel, and of election, those hearers who respond), and denies that any man's salvation is secured by any of them. The two theologies thus conceive the plan of salvation in quite different terms. One makes salvation depend on the work of God, the other on a work of man. . . .[1]

Table 8.1
The TULIP's Third Petal

1	**T**otal depravity	Humanity's radical corruption
2	**U**nconditional election	God's sovereign choice
3	**Limited atonement**	Christ's purposeful atonement
4	**I**rresistible grace	The Spirit's effective call
5	**P**erseverance of the saints	God's preservation of the saints

In the same essay Packer says the Arminian concept, as debated at the Synod of Dort in 1618, declares that "Christ's death did not ensure the salvation of anyone, for it did not secure the gift of faith to anyone (there is no such gift); what it did was rather to create a possibility of salvation for everyone if they believe."[2]

The question answered by the doctrine of limited atonement is this: Is Christ a real Savior or merely a "potential" Savior? The doctrine of limited atonement, the L of TULIP, is probably the most disputed term of the five. The idea that the atonement is "limited" provides the crux of the controversy. To state the question in another way: Did Christ die to atone for the sins of every human being, or did he die to atone for the sins of the elect only?

The atonement of Christ was clearly limited or unlimited. There is no alternative, no *tertium quid*. If it is unlimited in an absolute sense, then an atonement has been made for every person's sins. Christ has then made propitiation for all persons' sins and expiated them as well.

It seems to follow from the idea of unlimited atonement that salvation is universal. The vast majority of Arminians, Dispensationalists, and other semi-Pelagians who deny limited atonement, however, reject universalism. Historic Arminianism embraces particularism: not all people are saved, only a particular number of them. That particular group of people who are saved are those who respond to the offer of the gospel with faith. Only those who believe appropriate the benefits of the saving atonement in Christ. The person who fails to embrace the saving work of Christ with faith is ultimately left without the expiation of his sins, the propitiation of the cross, and the satisfaction of God's justice.

In this view faith is not only a condition for redemption, but also one of the very grounds of redemption. If the atonement is not efficacious apart from faith, then faith must be necessary for the satisfaction of divine justice. Here faith becomes a work with a vengeance because its presence or absence in a sinner determines the efficacy of Christ's work of satisfaction for this person.

I can hear the howls of protest from the Arminian camp. They steadfastly abhor the idea that human faith adds any "value" to the finished work of Christ or to the efficacy of Christ's work of satisfaction. The formula they normally use is that Christ's atonement is *sufficient* for all, but *efficient* only for some.

Reformed theologians do not question that the value of Christ's atonement is sufficient to cover the sins of the whole fallen race. The value of his sacrifice is unlimited. His merit is sufficient to cover the demerits of all who sin. We also agree that the atonement is efficient only for some, an idea that is integral to the doctrine of limited atonement.

When we speak of the sufficiency of the atonement, however, we must ask the question, Is it a sufficient satisfaction of divine justice? If it is sufficient to satisfy the demands of God's justice, then no one needs to worry about future punishment. If God accepts payment of one person's moral debt from another, will he then exact payment of the same debt later by the person himself? The answer is obviously no.

This means that if Christ really, objectively satisfied the demands of God's justice for everyone, then everyone will be saved. It is one thing to agree that faith is a necessary condition for the appropriation of the benefits of Christ's atoning work, for justification and its fruits. It is quite another to say that faith is a necessary condition for the satisfaction of divine justice. If faith is a condition for God's justice to be satisfied, then the atonement, in itself, is not sufficient to satisfy the demands of God's justice. In itself the atonement is not "sufficient" for anyone, let alone for all. Full satisfaction is not rendered until or unless a person adds to the atonement his faith.

Again Arminians will protest that they do not, in fact, make faith a work of satisfaction. Faith is a necessary condition, they say, not a work of satisfaction. But the question remains, Is divine satisfaction effected without faith? If so, then no satisfaction is left to be imposed on unrepentant sinners. If not, then faith is clearly an element necessary for satisfaction, an element that we supply.

The great Puritan theologian John Owen said this:

First, if the full debt of all be paid to the utmost extent of the obligation, how comes it to pass that so many are shut up in prison to eternity, never freed from their debts? Secondly, if the Lord, as a just creditor, ought to cancel all obligations and surcease all suits against such as have their debts so paid, whence is it that his wrath smokes against some to all eternity? Let none tell me that it is because they walk not worthy of the benefit bestowed; for that not walking worthy is part of the debt which is fully paid, for (as it is in the third inference) the debt so paid is all our sins. Thirdly, is it probable that God calls any to a second payment, and requires satisfaction of them for whom, by his own acknowledgment, Christ hath made that which is full and sufficient?[3]

Let me consider the benefit of Christ's atonement for me. I am presently a believer in Christ. Today I enjoy the benefit of an atonement made for me centuries ago. Did that atonement satisfy the demands of God's justice on all of my sins? If it did, then it satisfied the penalty for the sin of my previous unbelief. Was that sin paid for before I believed? Or was Christ's atonement not complete until I came to faith? Did his death cover my unbelief or not? If it did, why then does his atonement not cover the unbelief of unbelievers? It covers my *former* unbelief but not the *present* unbelief of unbelievers. Advocates of unlimited atonement say the sin of unbelief is not covered unless the condition of faith is met. My faith then makes Christ's atonement efficacious for me.

If faith is necessary to the atonement, then Christ's work was indeed a mere potentiality. In itself it saves no one. It merely makes salvation possible. Theoretically we must ask the obvious question, What would have happened to the work of Christ if nobody believed in it? That had to be a theoretical possibility. In this case Christ would have died in vain. He would have been a potential Savior of all but an actual Savior of none.

"That is pure speculation," the Arminian replies. The reality is that many have and do embrace Christ in faith. Christ is a bona fide Savior. People truly are saved by his work. Besides, when our omniscient God sent Christ into the world to make an atonement, he knew this would be no exercise in futility. The Father knew that not only would he be satisfied by the work of his Son, but the Son himself would see the travail of his own soul and be satisfied.

This divine satisfaction, however, would be limited. If God sent Christ to save everyone, then he must remain eternally dissatisfied with the results. Though the Son may receive satisfaction from knowing that some have availed themselves of his atonement, his satisfaction must be partial because so many have not.

This raises the cardinal point in the doctrine of limited atonement. The ultimate question has to do not so much with the sufficiency or efficiency of the atonement, but with its *design*. What was God's original purpose or intent in sending his Son into the world? Was his divine plan to make redemption possible or to make it certain?

If God planned to redeem all men, did his plan fail? Did God know in advance who would believe and who would not? Was the faith of believers part of his plan?

Our answers to these questions all depend on our understanding of God's character, of his sovereignty and omniscience.

God's Will and Redemption

The Bible says God is "not willing that any should perish" (2 Pet. 3:9). What does this passage mean? There are at least three different ways to interpret it, and they cannot all be correct. The first problem is the meaning of the word *willing*. The Bible speaks of the will of God in several ways. The most frequent usages refer to (1) his decretive will, (2) his preceptive will, and (3) his will of disposition.

The *decretive will* is sometimes referred to as God's sovereign, efficacious will, by which what he decrees must necessarily come to pass. If God decrees sovereignly that something will happen, it will certainly take place. The decretive will is irresistible.

The *preceptive will* refers to God's precepts or commands, the law he enjoins upon his creatures. We are able to violate his preceptive will. That is, we are capable of sinning, of disobeying his law. We may not do it with impunity, but we are able to do it. This is a classic case of the difference between *may* and *can*. *Can* refers to ability, while *may* refers to positive permission.

Table 8.2
The Will of God

Decretive will	The sovereign, efficacious will of God	Cannot be resisted
Preceptive will	The precepts, commands of God	Can be resisted
Will of disposition	That which pleases, delights God	Can be resisted

The *will of disposition*, referred to in Scripture, means that which is pleasing or delightful to God.

If we apply these different concepts of the will of God to 2 Peter 3:9, we get different results:

1. God is not willing (in the sovereign, decretive sense) that any should perish. This means every person will be redeemed. No person will ever perish.

   This interpretation proves more than the Arminian or semi-Pelagian wants. It establishes universalism, which puts this text on a collision course with everything the Bible teaches about particularism.

2. God is not willing (in the preceptive sense) that any should perish. This means God forbids, in a moral sense, anyone to perish. To perish is an act of disobedience or a sin.

   Now surely anyone who in fact does perish does so as a law-breaker and is guilty of manifold acts of disobedience. It is possible to interpret the text in this manner, but it is a highly unlikely choice. It jars the mind to say that the text means merely that God does not "allow" people to perish.

3. God is not willing (in the dispositional sense) that any should perish. This means virtually the same thing as other texts, for example, those that say God does not delight in the death of the wicked. This speaks of God's common grace and general love or benevolence for mankind. A human judge who sentences a guilty person to prison does not enjoy this task. He takes no gleeful delight in meting out punishment, yet he performs the task in order to uphold justice. We know that God is not full of glee when a wicked person dies, yet he still wills that death in some sense. Nor does this mean that God does something he really does not want to do. God wanted his Son to die on the cross. He ordained, willed, and commanded it. In

one sense it pleased God to bruise his Son. His divine pleasure came, not from inflicting his wrath on his beloved Son, but from bringing about redemption. Of these three options, this one fits the whole context of Scripture the best.

We need to pay more attention, however, to the term *any*. *Any* can refer to (1) any person in a universal class or (2) any person in a particular class. The text apparently makes no explicit restriction to a particular class. For this reason many conclude that *any* refers to the unrestricted universal class of human beings (though this itself is a restriction because it excludes angels and animals).

The full text, however, does include a restrictive term: "The Lord is long-suffering to us, not willing that any should perish, but that all should come to repentance." The restrictive word is *us*. *Any* refers to "any of us." This does not solve the problem instantly, however, for *us* may refer to us human beings (universally) or to a particular group of us. Since 2 Peter is written by a Christian believer to Christian believers and for Christian believers, it is likely that *us* refers to Christian believers. John Owen writes:

> Who are these of whom the apostle speaks, to whom he writes? Such as had received "great and precious promises" (2 Pet. 1:4), whom he calls "beloved" (2 Pet. 3:1); whom he opposeth to the "scoffers" of the "last days" (2 Pet. 3:3); to whom the Lord hath respect in the disposal of these days; who are said to be "elect" (Matt. 24:22). Now, truly, to argue that because God would have none of those to perish, but all of them to come to repentance, therefore he hath the same will and mind towards all and every one

in the world (even those to whom he never makes known his will, nor ever calls to repentance, if they never once hear of his way of salvation), comes not much short of extreme madness and folly.[4]

Owen's point is that *us* refers to God's elect, so God is not willing that any of his elect should perish. In this case the text must refer to the will of God in the decretive sense. God sovereignly decrees that none of his elect shall perish. As a result the goal of election is assured. All of the elect come to repentance. All of the elect come to faith. All of the elect are saved. None of the elect perish. This is indeed the very purpose of election, and this purpose is not frustrated.

God's decree of election is a sovereign decree. It is fully efficacious. All that is necessary for the elect to be saved is brought to pass sovereignly by God.

God's Omniscience

God's omniscience refers to God's total knowledge of all things actual and potential. God knows not only all that is, but everything that possibly could be. The expert chess player exemplifies a kind of omniscience, though it is limited to the options of chess play. He knows that his opponent can make move A, B, C, or D, and so forth. Each possible move opens up certain countermoves. The more moves ahead the expert can consider, the more he can control his chess-game destiny. The more options and counter-options one considers, the more complex and difficult the reasoning.

In reality no chess player is omniscient. God knows not only all available options, but also which option will be exercised. He knows the end before the beginning. God's omniscience excludes both ignorance and learning. If there is ignorance in the mind of God, then divine omniscience is a hollow, indeed fraudulent, phrase. Learning always presupposes a certain level of ignorance. One simply cannot learn what one already knows. There is no learning curve for God. Since no gaps exist in his knowledge, there is nothing for him to learn.

For us to know what will happen tomorrow, we must guess concerning things that are contingent. If I say to a friend, "What are you going to do tomorrow?" he might reply, "That depends." Those two words acknowledge that there are contingencies ahead and that what happens to us depends on these contingencies.

It is said that God knows all contingencies, but none of them contingently. God never says to himself, "That depends." Nothing is contingent to him. He knows all things that will happen because he ordains everything that does happen. This is crucial to our understanding of God's omniscience. He does not know what will happen by virtue of exceedingly good guesswork about future events. He knows it with certainty because he has decreed it.

The *Westminster Confession* avers: "God from all eternity, did, by the most wise and holy counsel of His own will, freely, and unchangeably ordain whatsoever comes to pass. . . ."[5]

This statement refers to God's eternal and immutable decretive will. It applies to everything that happens. Does this mean that *everything* that happens is the will of God? Yes. Augustine qualified this answer by adding the words, "in a certain sense." That is, God ordains "in some sense" everything that happens. Nothing that takes place is beyond the scope of his sovereign will. The movement of every molecule, the actions of every plant, the falling of every star, the choices of every volitional creature, all of these are subject to his sovereign will. No maverick molecules run loose in the universe, beyond the control of the Creator. If one such molecule existed, it could be the critical fly in the eternal ointment. As one grain of sand in the kidney of Oliver Cromwell changed the course of English history, so one maverick molecule could destroy every promise God has ever made about the outcome of history.

The "certain sense" of which Augustine spoke has often been articulated by a distinction between God's *decretive will* and his *permissive will*. This distinction is valid if used properly, but it is fraught with peril. It hints at a false dichotomy. The distinction is not absolute: what God permits, he *decrees* to permit. For example, at any given moment of my life, God has the power and authority to intrude providentially and to restrain my actions. In a word he can *prevent* me from sinning if he so chooses. If he chooses not to prevent me, he has clearly chosen to "permit" me to sin. This permission is not a divine sanction on my behavior. That he permits me to sin merely means that he chooses to allow it to happen rather than to intrude and prevent it. Because he chooses to let it happen, in some sense he ordains or intends that it should happen.

This reflects God's *passive* decree, which is *active* with respect to his *intention*, but passive with respect to his action. We see this in the doctrine of providential concurrence: the intentions of two parties, God and man, flow together in a single event. The clearest biblical example of this can be found in the narrative about Joseph and his brothers. The treachery of his brothers did not fall outside of God's sovereign ordination. Joseph said to his brothers: "You meant evil against me; but God meant it for good, in order to bring it about as it is this day, to save many people alive" (Gen. 50:20).

After the *Westminster Confession* speaks of God's ordaining whatever comes to pass, it adds: "yet so, as thereby neither is God the author of sin, nor is violence offered to the will of the creatures; nor is the liberty or contingency of second causes taken away, but rather established."[6]

"Second causes" are *secondary*, and as such are dependent on a *primary* cause for their potency. God, and God alone, is the sole *primary cause* in the universe. He is not merely the first cause in the Aristotelian sense of the first in a long chain of causes. He is the *ground* of all causal power. Scripture declares that in God "we live and move and have our being" (Acts 17:28). God is the ground of all being, all life, and all motion. Apart from his power to create and sustain life, no life is possible. Apart from his power of being, nothing else would be or could be. Apart from his power of motion (primary causality), nothing can move, change, act, or bring about effects. God is not like Aristotle's *unmoved mover*. Will Durant once likened Aristotle's god to the King of England: he reigns but does not rule. God not only reigns, but also rules, and he rules sovereignly.

Secondary causes are not, however, imaginary or impotent. They exert real causal power. We make real choices. Yet a secondary cause is always dependent on the primary cause, God himself, for its efficacy.

God brings to pass his sovereign will through or by means of secondary causes. "By means of" is another way of saying that God ordains not only the *ends*, but also the *means* to these ends.

The doctrine of limited atonement hinges on the specific design or end for which Christ went to the cross. John Owen remarks: "By the end of the death of Christ, we mean in general, both . . . that which his Father and himself intended *in* it; and . . . that which was effectually fulfilled and accomplished *by* it."[7]

The goal of the atonement was to save the lost. Christ loved his church and gave himself for it. He died in order to save his sheep. His purpose was to effect reconciliation and redemption for his people.

The Father's ultimate purpose was to save the elect. He designed the Son's atonement to accomplish the goal or end of redemption. Every Arminian would agree with that. The issue is this: Was God's purpose to make salvation for all possible, or to make salvation for the elect certain? The ultimate aim of God's plan of redemption was to redeem his elect. To accomplish this end he ordained the means. One was the atonement made by his Son. Another was the Holy Spirit's application of this atonement to the elect. God provides for his elect all that is necessary for their salvation, including the gift of faith.

Once we grasp the doctrine of total depravity, we know that no person will incline himself to faith in the atoning work of Christ.

If God does not supply the means of appropriating the atonement's benefits, namely faith, then the potential redemption of all would result in the actual redemption of none.

The Intercession of Christ

The atonement is Christ's chief work as our great High Priest, but it is not his only priestly task. He also lives as our intercessor with the Father. His intercession is another means to the end or purpose of the elect's redemption. Christ not only dies for his sheep, but also prays for them. His special work of intercession is definite in its design. In his high priestly prayer Jesus says:

> I have manifested Your name to the men whom You have given Me out of the world. They were Yours, You gave them to Me, and they have kept Your word. Now they have known that all things which You have given Me are from You. . . . I pray for them. I do not pray for the world but for those whom You have given Me, for they are Yours. And all Mine are Yours, and Yours are Mine, and I am glorified in them. . . . Holy Father, keep through Your name those whom You have given Me, that they may be one as We are. While I was with them in the world, I kept them in Your name. Those whom You gave Me I have kept; and none of them is lost except the son of perdition, that the Scripture might be fulfilled. (John 17:6–12)

Jesus intercedes here in behalf of those whom the Father has given him. It is abundantly clear that this does not include all mankind. The Father gave to Christ a *limited* number of people. They are the ones for whom Christ prays. They are also the ones for whom Christ died. Jesus does not pray for the whole world. He says that directly and clearly. He prays specifically for the ones given to him, the elect.

Earlier in John's Gospel Jesus says: "All that the Father gives Me will come to Me, and the one who comes to Me I will by no means cast out. For I have come down from heaven, not to do My own will, but the will of Him who sent Me. This is the will of the Father who sent Me, that of all He has given Me I should lose nothing, but should raise it up at the last day" (6:37–39). There is no uncertainty here. The work of redemption accomplished by Christ as our surety is no mere possibility or potentiality. It is a certainty.

That Christ does not pray for the whole world and does not die for the whole world is disputed by semi-Pelagians of all sorts. The most important text to which they appeal is found in the First Epistle of John: "If anyone sins, we have an Advocate with the Father, Jesus Christ the righteous. And He Himself is the propitiation for our sins, and not for ours only but also for the whole world" (2:1–2). On the surface this text seems to demolish limited atonement, saying explicitly that Christ is the propitiation of the sins for the "whole world." The whole world is set in contrast with "our." We must ask, What does *our* mean here, and what does *whole world* mean here?

Our could refer to Christians as distinguished from non-Christians, believers as opposed to nonbelievers. If this interpretation is correct, then Christ is a propitiation not only for Christian believers, but for everybody in the whole world.

On the other hand *our* could refer specifically to Jewish believers. One of the central questions of the church's earliest formative period was this: Who is to be included in the

New Covenant community? The New Testament labors the point that the body of Christ includes not only ethnic Jews, but also Samaritans and Gentiles. The church is composed of people from every tribe and nation, from people drawn out of the whole world, not merely the world of Israel.

Ample evidence indicates that the term *world* in the New Testament often refers to neither the entire globe nor to all persons living on earth. For example, we read this in Luke: "It came to pass in those days that a decree went out from Caesar Augustus that all the world should be registered" (2:1). We know this census did not include the inhabitants of China or South America, so "all the world" does not refer to all people in the entire world. The usage of *world* in this manner is widespread in Scripture.

Semi-Pelagians also appeal to 2 Corinthians, where Paul says that "God was in Christ reconciling the world to Himself, not imputing their trespasses to them, and has committed to us the word of reconciliation" (5:19). Paul speaks of Christ's "reconciling the world" to God in the indicative mood. Moments later he switches from the indicative to the imperative: "Be reconciled to God" (5:20). Is this a command simply to be what we already are?

To be sure, Christ's propitiation on the cross is unlimited in its sufficiency or value. In this sense Christ makes an atonement for the whole world. But the efficacy of this atonement does not apply to the whole world, nor does its ultimate design.

The atonement's ultimate purpose is found in the ultimate purpose or will of God. This purpose or design does not include the entire human race. If it did, the entire human race would surely be redeemed.

9

THE SPIRIT'S EFFECTIVE CALL

The concept of irresistible grace, the I in TULIP, is closely linked to the doctrines of regeneration and effectual calling.

When John H. Gerstner was a college student, he took a course in theology from John Orr, one of the nation's most learned and distinguished scholars in the early twentieth century. During one lecture Orr wrote on the blackboard in large letters: **Regeneration precedes faith**. These words stunned Gerstner. He was sure his professor had made a mistake and unintentionally reversed the order of the words. Did not every Christian know that faith is a necessary prerequisite for regeneration, that one must believe in Christ to be born again?

Table 9.1
The TULIP's Fourth Petal

1	**T**otal depravity	Humanity's radical corruption
2	**U**nconditional election	God's sovereign choice
3	**L**imited atonement	Christ's purposeful atonement
4	**Irresistible grace**	The Spirit's effective call
5	**P**erseverance of the saints	God's preservation of the saints

This was John Gerstner's virgin exposure to Reformed theology, and it startled him. That regeneration comes before faith, not after it or as a result of it, was an idea he had never considered. Once he heard his professor's cogent argument, Gerstner was convinced and his life was set on an entirely different course.

This tends to be something of a pattern for Calvinists. As Roger Nicole declared, "We are all born Pelagians." Conversion to Christ does not instantly cure us of our Pelagian tendencies. From the earliest days of our conversion, our Pelagianism is reinforced on every side. We brought it with us out of paganism, and the secular world around us reinforces it with the humanistic view of human freedom and inherent goodness. In the church we are widely exposed to Arminianism, which has had American evangelicalism in a stranglehold since the days of Charles Finney.

During the controversy over justification in the sixteenth century, Martin Luther wrote a controversial work entitled *The Babylonian Captivity of the Church*. This book likened the Roman Catholic church to pagan Babylon of antiquity. If Luther were alive today, I suspect he would write a book entitled *The Pelagian Captivity of the Church*. Though Arminianism is more properly speaking a variety of semi-Pelagianism, the "semi" is a thin patina. The essence of Pelagianism is retained in semi-Pelagianism, and it is carried through into Arminianism and, to a degree, into Dispensationalism.

The introductory essay to a current edition of *Bondage of the Will* asks what the modern reader should make of Luther's classic:

> That it is a brilliant and exhilarating performance, a masterpiece of the controversialist's difficult art, he will no doubt readily admit; but now comes the question, is Luther's case any part of God's truth? and, if so, has it a message for Christians to-day? No doubt the reader will find the way by which Luther leads him to be a strange new road, an approach which in all probability he has never considered, a line of thought which he would normally label "Calvinistic" and hastily pass by. This is what Lutheran orthodoxy itself has done; and the present-day Evangelical Christian (who has semi-Pelagianism in his blood) will be inclined to do the same. But both history and Scripture, if allowed to speak, counsel otherwise.[1]

From the vantage point of the twentieth century, it appears that the central issue of the Reformation was the doctrine of justification. To a degree this is an accurate assessment. But behind and beneath the doctrine of justification was the deeper concern of the graciousness of our salvation, wrought entirely by God himself and by no human achievement whatever.

> Historically, it is a simple matter of fact that Martin Luther and John Calvin, and, for that matter, Ulrich Zwingli, Martin Bucer, and all the leading Protestant theologians of the first epoch of the Reformation, stood on precisely

the same ground here. On other points, they had their differences; but in asserting the helplessness of man in sin, and the sovereignty of God in grace, they were entirely at one. To all of them, these doctrines were the very life-blood of the Christian faith. A modern editor of Luther's great work underscores this fact: "Whoever puts this book down without having realised that evangelical theology stands or falls with the doctrine of the bondage of the will has read it in vain."[2]

Simply because a theologian, even a highly respected one, declares that evangelical theology "stands or falls" with its view of the human will does not make it so. This scholar may be using hyperbole, like the proverbial board on the mule's head, to gain our attention. Hyperbole involves the use of intentional exaggeration to make a point.

This is not hyperbole. In the judgment of the magisterial Reformers themselves, one's view of the will and its state of bondage is absolutely vital to one's understanding of the entire Christian faith. Luther himself said:

This is the hinge on which our discussion turns, the crucial issue between us; our aim is, simply, to investigate what ability "free will" has, in what respect it is the subject of Divine action and how it stands related to the grace of God. If we know nothing of these things, we shall know nothing whatsoever of Christianity, and shall be in worse case than any people on earth! He who dissents from that statement should acknowledge that he is no Christian; and he who ridicules or derides it should realise that he is the Christian's chief foe. For if I am ignorant of the nature, extent and limits of what I can and must do with reference to God, I shall be equally ignorant and uncertain of the nature, extent and limits of what God can and will do in me—though God, in fact, works all in all (cf. 1 Cor. 12:6). Now, if I am ignorant of God's works and power, I am ignorant of God himself; and if I do not know God, I cannot worship, praise, give thanks or serve Him, for I do not know how much I should attribute to myself and how much to Him. We need, therefore, to have in mind a clear-cut distinction between God's power and ours, and God's work and ours, if we would live a godly life.[3]

It is often assumed that the chief issue of the Reformation was the issue of justification. Luther hurled his thunderbolts at every form of human merit. Together the Reformers clearly saw the link between the doctrine of justification and the primacy of grace:

The doctrine of justification by faith was important to them because it safeguarded the principle of sovereign grace; but it actually expressed for them only one aspect of this principle, and that not its deepest aspect. The sovereignty of grace found expression in their thinking at a profounder level still, in the doctrine of monergistic regeneration—the doctrine, that is, that the faith which receives Christ for justification is itself the free gift of a sovereign God, bestowed by spiritual regeneration in the act of effectual calling. To the Reformers, the crucial question was not simply, whether God justifies believers without works of law. It was the broader question, whether sinners are wholly helpless in their sin, and whether God is to be thought of as saving them by free, unconditional, invincible grace, not only justifying them for Christ's sake when they come to faith, but also raising them from the death of sin by His quickening Spirit in order to bring them to faith.[4]

So important to the Reformers was the issue of our total dependency on grace for salvation that they saw all forms of semi-Pelagianism as serious threats to the gospel:

> Is our salvation wholly of God, or does it ultimately depend on something that we do for ourselves? Those who say the latter (as the Arminians later did) thereby deny man's utter helplessness in sin, and affirm that a form of semi-Pelagianism is true after all. It is no wonder, then, that later Reformed theology condemned Arminianism as being in principle a return to Rome (because in effect it turned faith into a meritorious work) and a betrayal of the Reformation (because it denied the sovereignty of God in saving sinners, which was the deepest religious and theological principle of the Reformers' thought). Arminianism was, indeed, in Reformed eyes a renunciation of New Testament Christianity in favour of New Testament Judaism; for to rely on oneself for faith is no different in principle from relying on oneself for works, and the one is as un-Christian and anti-Christian as the other.[5]

Monergistic Regeneration

The doctrine of justification by faith alone was debated during the Reformation on the deeper level of monergistic regeneration. This technical term must be explained. *Monergism* is derived from a combination of a prefix and a root. The prefix *mono* is used frequently in English to indicate that which is single or alone. The root comes from the verb "to work." The *erg* of monergy comes into our language to indicate a unit of work or energy. When we put the prefix and root together, we get *monergy* or *monergism.* Monergism is something that operates by itself or works alone as the sole active party.

Monergism is the opposite of *synergism. Synergism* shares a common root with *monergism,* but it has a different prefix. The prefix *syn* comes from a Greek word meaning "with." Synergism is a cooperative venture, a working together of two or more parties.

When the term *monergism* is linked with the word *regeneration,* the phrase describes an action by which God the Holy Spirit works on a human being without this person's assistance or cooperation. This grace of regeneration may be called *operative grace. Cooperative grace,* on the other hand, is grace that God offers to sinners and that they may accept or reject, depending on the sinner's disposition.

Monergistic regeneration is exclusively a divine act. Man does not have the creative power God has. To quicken a person who is spiritually dead is something only God can do. A corpse cannot revive itself. It cannot even assist in the effort. It can only respond after receiving new life. Not only *can* it respond then, it most certainly *will* respond. In regeneration the soul of man is utterly passive until it has been made alive. It offers no help in reviving itself, though once revived it is empowered to act and respond.

Perhaps a good illustration of monergistic, life-giving power is the raising of Lazarus from the dead, a story told in the Gospel of John:

> Then Jesus, again groaning in Himself, came to the tomb. It was a cave, and a stone lay against it. Jesus said, "Take away the stone." Martha, the sister of him who was dead, said to Him, "Lord, by this time there is a stench, for he has been dead four days." Jesus said to

her, "Did I not say to you that if you would believe you would see the glory of God?" Then they took away the stone from the place where the dead man was lying. And Jesus lifted up His eyes and said, "Father, I thank You that You have heard Me. And I know that You always hear Me, but because of the people who are standing by I said this, that they may believe that You sent Me." Now when He had said these things, He cried with a loud voice, "Lazarus, come forth!" And he who had died came out bound hand and foot with graveclothes, and his face was wrapped with a cloth. Jesus said to them, "Loose him, and let him go."

Then many of the Jews who had come to Mary, and had seen the things Jesus did, believed in Him. But some of them went away to the Pharisees and told them the things Jesus did. (11:38–46)

Lazarus was dead, not critically ill or at the point of dying. He was already a corpse and was decomposing. The stench from his rotting body was repugnant to his sister Martha. The miracle of his resurrection was accomplished without means, that is, without balms, medicines, CPR, and so forth. The only power Christ used here was the power of his voice. He uttered a command, not a request or an invitation. He made no attempt to woo Lazarus from the tomb. This resurrection was strictly monergistic. Lazarus rendered absolutely no assistance. He was incapable of assisting in any way because he was completely dead.

Some may argue that though Christ supplied the initial power of Lazarus's resurrection, Lazarus nevertheless had to respond to Christ's command to come forth from the tomb. Is this not a cooperative work, a synergism between Christ and Lazarus? Most of the confusion regarding regeneration enters the picture here. Obviously Lazarus did respond. He came out of the tomb in obedience to Jesus's command. After life flowed anew in Lazarus's body, he became quite active.

Monergistic regeneration has to do, not with the whole process of redemption, but strictly with the initial condition or first step of our coming to faith. To be sure, Lazarus acted. He responded. He came forth from the tomb. But the crucial point is that he did none of these things while he was still dead. He did not respond to the call of Christ until after he had been made alive. His resurrection preceded his coming forth from the tomb. His restoration to life preceded his response.

Arminians do not appreciate this analogy and protest that we are here comparing apples and oranges. Obviously in the case of physical death, a corpse cannot respond or cooperate. It has no power to respond because it is dead. But there is a difference between physical death and spiritual death. A physically dead person can do nothing either physically or spiritually. A spiritually dead person is still alive biologically. This person can still act, work, respond, make decisions, and so forth. He can say yes to grace, or he can say no.

Here we reach the ultimate point of separation between semi-Pelagianism and Augustinianism, between Arminianism and Calvinism, between Rome and the Reformation. Here we discover whether we are utterly dependent on grace for our salvation or if, while still in the flesh, still in bondage to sin, and still dead in sin, we can cooperate with grace in such a way that affects our eternal destiny.

In the Reformation view, the work of regeneration is performed by God and by him alone. The sinner is completely passive in receiving this action. Regeneration is an example of operative grace. Any cooperation we display toward God occurs only *after* the work of regeneration has been completed. Of course we respond to this work. We respond in a manner similar to that of Lazarus when, after being loosed, he stepped out of the tomb.

In like manner we step out of our tombs of spiritual death. We also respond when we hear the call of Christ. Our regeneration does not preclude such a response, but is designed to make this response not only possible but certain. The point is, however, that unless we first receive the grace of regeneration, we will not and cannot respond to the gospel in a positive way. Regeneration must occur first before there can be any positive response of faith.

Arminianism reverses the order of salvation. It has faith preceding regeneration. The sinner, who is dead in sin and in bondage to sin, must somehow shed his chains, revive his spiritual vitality, and exercise faith so that he or she may be born again. In a very real sense regeneration is not so much a gift in this schema as it is a reward for responding to the offer of grace. The Arminian argues that in this schema grace is primary, in that God first offers grace for regeneration. God takes the initiative. He makes the first move and takes the first step. But this step is not decisive. This step may be thwarted by the sinner. If the sinner refuses to cooperate with or assent to this proffered grace, then grace is to no avail.

Resistible Grace

There is a crucial difference between pure Pelagianism and semi-Pelagianism. In pure Pelagianism grace may facilitate salvation, but it is by no means necessary for it. A person can be saved without grace, either operative or cooperative. In semi-Pelagianism grace is not only helpful for salvation but necessary for it. Grace is necessary to assist the sinner in responding positively to God. Grace is necessary, but not necessarily effectual. Grace may be resisted and overcome.

In the final analysis semi-Pelagianism removes the odious problem of Pelagianism, but only by one step. Semi-Pelagianism salutes the necessity of grace, but under close scrutiny one wonders if the difference between Pelagianism and semi-Pelagianism is a distinction without a difference.

The problem is this: If grace is necessary but not effectual, what makes it work? Obviously it is the positive response of the sinner, who is still in the flesh. Why does one sinner respond to the offer of grace positively and the other negatively? Is the difference in response found in the power of the human will or in some added measure of grace? Does grace assist the sinner in cooperating with grace, or does the sinner cooperate by the power of the flesh alone? If the latter, it is unvarnished Pelagianism. If the former, it is still Pelagianism in that grace merely facilitates regeneration and salvation.

"No, no, no," cries the semi-Pelagian. "Sproul has missed the point entirely. Semi-Pelagianism rejects pure Pelagianism at the point of saying that grace is necessary for salvation, not merely helpful."

We know this is what semi-Pelagians say, but how in fact does this work out in their understanding of regeneration? If the flesh can, by itself, incline itself to grace, where is the need of grace? If the grace of regeneration is merely offered and its efficacy depends on the sinner's response, what does grace accomplish that is not already present in the power of the flesh?

What the unregenerate person desperately needs in order to come to faith is regeneration. This is the necessary grace. It is the *sine qua non* of salvation. Unless God changes the disposition of my sinful heart, I will never choose to cooperate with grace or embrace Christ in faith. These are the very things to which the flesh is indisposed. If God merely *offers* to change my heart, what will that accomplish for me as long as my heart remains opposed to him? If he offers me grace while I am a slave to sin and still in the flesh, what good is the offer? Saving grace does not *offer* liberation, it liberates. Saving grace does not merely offer regeneration, it regenerates. This is what makes grace so gracious: God unilaterally and monergistically does for us what we cannot do for ourselves.

The phrase *irresistible grace*, like others that make up the acrostic TULIP, can be misleading. TULIP stands for total depravity, unconditional election, limited atonement, irresistible grace, and perseverance of the saints. If we adjusted these phrases in the interest of accuracy, we would have something like this: radical corruption, sovereign election, definite atonement, effectual grace, and preservation of the saints. This would give us the acrostic RSDEP. This seems such a waste of tulips that we will stay with the original acrostic and simply labor the clarifications necessary.

Irresistible grace is not irresistible in the sense that sinners are incapable of resisting it. Though the sinner is spiritually dead, he remains biologically alive and kicking. As Scripture suggests, the sinner always resists the Holy Spirit. We are so opposed to the grace of God that we do everything in our power to resist it. *Irresistible grace* means that the sinner's resistance to the grace of regeneration cannot thwart the Spirit's purpose. The grace of regeneration is irresistible in the sense that it is invincible.

Since the grace of regeneration is monergistic and requires no cooperation from us, its efficacy lies in itself and not in us. We can do nothing to make it effective; we can do nothing to make it ineffective. We are as passive with respect to our own regeneration as Lazarus was to his resurrection, and as the universe was to its creation. We were not cooperating agents in our original biological conception or generation, nor are we active agents in our regeneration.

The doctrine of irresistible grace is so called because of its monergistic action and efficacy. Historically it has been called effectual calling.

Effectual Calling

The Westminster Confession of Faith devotes an entire chapter to the doctrine of effectual calling. It begins by declaring:

> All those whom God has predestined unto life, and those only, He is pleased, in His appointed and accepted time, effectually to call, by His Word and Spirit, out of that state of sin and death, in which they are by nature to

grace and salvation, by Jesus Christ; enlightening their minds spiritually and savingly to understand the things of God, taking away their heart of stone, and giving unto them an heart of flesh; renewing their wills, and, by His almighty power, determining them to that which is good, and effectually drawing them to Jesus Christ: yet so, as they come most freely, being made willing by His grace.[6]

Effectual calling is effectual because in it and by it God effects exactly what he intends in the operation: the quickening of spiritually dead souls to spiritual life. *Calling* refers to the Holy Spirit's inward or secret operation on the soul. The confession's metaphor of turning a heart of stone into a heart of flesh is drawn directly from Scripture. The image may be a bit confusing because of the positive reference to the word *flesh*.

In the Bible *flesh* usually refers to our fallen nature, which stands in contrast with and in opposition to the Spirit. In this image, however, *flesh* is not contrasted with spirit but with a stone. The same point is in view in both sets of images, namely a transformation from death to life. Apart from the grace of regeneration, the person's heart or soul is, with respect to the things of God, like a stone. It is inert, unfeeling, unresponsive. It is reified and calcified. It is called stony because it is morally hard. The heart of stone is also a heart of darkness, lacking both life and light.

The grace of regeneration changes the heart or soul from something cold, lifeless, and stony into something living, pulsating, sanguine, and responsive. The heart is "made alive" to the things of God. Calvin quotes Augustine as saying: "This grace, which is secretly imparted to the hearts of men, is not received by any hard heart; for the reason for which it is given is, that the hardness of the heart may first be taken away. Hence, when the Father is heard within, he takes away the stony heart, and gives a heart of flesh. Thus he makes them sons of promise and vessels of mercy, which he has prepared for glory."[7]

God's call is made effectual by the Word and the Spirit. It is important to see that Word and Spirit are here conjoined as two vital factors in regeneration. The Holy Spirit is not working apart from the Word or against the Word, but with the Word. Nor is the Word working alone without the presence and power of the Spirit.

The call referred to in effectual calling is not the outward call of the gospel that can be heard by anyone within range of the preaching. The call referred to here is the *inward call*, the call that penetrates to and pierces the heart, quickening it to spiritual life. Hearing the gospel enlightens the mind, yet it does not awaken the soul until the Holy Spirit illumines and regenerates it. The move from ear to soul is made by the Holy Spirit. This move is what accomplishes God's purpose of applying the benefits of Christ's work to the elect.

The *Westminster Confession* speaks of the Spirit's renewing the will and of determining it to what is good by his almighty power. This refers to the omnipotence of God. Far from a mere enticement, God's effectual call on the human soul derives from the power source of omnipotence. The same power that called the world into existence out of nothing is now exercised in our redemption. As God calls the world into being out of nothing, so he calls us to saving faith out of "nothing," calling us who have no spiritual virtue whatever.

The confession speaks of God's determination. This is not to be confused with the blind determinism of fate or of mechanical physical forces. This is the determination of an omnipotent and holy Being, who is determined to bring about the salvation of his elect. God is determined to accomplish his plan, and by his determinate counsel that is exactly what he does.

In the phrase *effectual calling*, the stress is on the word *effectual*. The confession speaks of God's drawing the sinner to Christ, borrowing the word *draw* from Scripture but qualifying it with the adverb *effectually*. The Holy Spirit's drawing is effectual; it accomplishes its purpose.

The effect of this inward calling on the sinner is real. Regeneration and effectual calling effect a real change in the person. He is not merely induced to a particular action that he otherwise might not take. Regeneration produces a real and substantive change in the person's constituent nature. His will is renewed and liberated. He is freed from the bondage of original sin. He receives a new disposition for the things of God. Saving faith is worked in the heart. As a result of regeneration, the person becomes a new creature.

Regeneration and Dispensationalism

Shortly after the publication of John H. Gerstner's book *Wrongly Dividing the Word of Truth*,[8] I received inquiries from Dispensational friends who were disturbed by the sharpness of his critique and by his charge that Dispensational theology is "dubious" evangelicalism. Gerstner labored to show that the alleged Calvinism of

Dispensationalism is spurious. He hammered away at the inherent antinomianism built into the Dispensational view of grace and law. He stressed the deficiencies in Dispensationalism's doctrine of sanctification, which has engendered so much controversy with respect to the Lordship of Christ. I had written the foreword to Gerstner's book, and this seemed to cause my friends more distress than the book itself.

A friend who teaches at Dallas Theological Seminary called me by phone and asked in a most gracious, earnest manner what I think is the most serious issue dividing Dispensationalism and Reformed theology. I answered that the most significant difference, at least in the long run because of its impact on theology as a whole, may be the different views of regeneration. According to Dispensationalism when the Holy Spirit regenerates a person, nothing really happens to effect change in the person's constituent nature.

In the Dispensational view, the Holy Spirit indwells the believer but may or may not change the believer's nature. The believer must cooperate with the indwelling Spirit to effect the changes that should accompany sanctification. This makes it possible for the believer to be in a state of grace and remain a "carnal Christian," one who receives Jesus as Savior but not as Lord. Though the believer *should* embrace Christ as both Savior and Lord, it is possible for the believer to submit to Christ only as Savior.

There is an intramural debate among Dispensationalists on this point. Some argue that the believer will inevitably submit to Christ as Lord, but not necessarily immediately. The person may, at least for a time, remain carnal. They appeal to the New Testament, in which Paul calls himself carnal and believers are sometimes addressed as "carnal." To be carnal is to be "fleshy," to act according to the old nature and not the new nature.

The issue is not whether Christians sin or at times act in a carnal manner. The issue is whether one can be completely carnal and be regenerate at the same time. Some Dispensationalists believe that one can be completely carnal and still be a Christian. This presupposes that regeneration does not necessarily involve a change in the person's constituent nature. Something is added to the human nature, namely the indwelling presence of the Holy Spirit. But the Spirit may cohabit with the sinner and never change his nature. The sinner may continue to be utterly carnal, with his personal nature unchanged.

The Reformed objection to Dispensationalism's carnal-Christian theory is based on the Reformed doctrine of regeneration. What is generated anew is the person's nature. The heart of the sinner is truly changed. Once in bondage to sin, the sinner is now liberated unto newness of life. The fruit of obedience is both inevitable and necessary; it is immediate. Obedience is by no means perfect, nor does it in any way contribute to the ground of one's justification. Its absence, however, points to the absence of regeneration. A totally carnal person is an unregenerate person, and an unregenerate person is an unsaved person.

Often lurking in the background of this dispute is a semi-Pelagian view of salvation. Though Dispensationalists claim to be "four-point Calvinists," some reject, in addition to the L of TULIP, the I.

Let us look briefly at the teaching of Dispensational-ist Zane C. Hodges, who has been at the center of the Lordship-salvation controversy. Hodges writes in his book *Absolutely Free*: "It is the consistent testimony of the New Testament Scriptures that God's Word in the gospel is what produces the miracle of regeneration. It—and it alone—is the powerful, life-giving seed which takes root in the human heart when that Word is received there in faith."[9]

Hodges makes it clear that regeneration is a miracle. It is accomplished by the power of God, not by human strength. The question is, however, *when* does this miracle take place? According to Hodges it occurs when the Word is received in faith. Faith precedes regeneration and is the necessary condition for it. This places Hodges squarely in the semi-Pelagian camp. Later Hodges says: "And what happens to those who appropriate that water ['the water of life']? What happens to those who believe this invitation ['Let him take the water of life freely' (Rev. 22:17)]? A *miracle* happens to them. They are born again. New life is imparted to them. And in the possession of that life, they possess also God's Son (1 John 5:12). Indeed, *He is that life* (1 John 5:20c), and thus He Himself lives within them (Col. 1:27)."[10]

Hodges summarizes his view:

What really happens when a person believes the saving Word of the gospel? There are numerous answers to this question. . . . But at least two things are so utterly funda-mental that they must never be forgotten.

One is that a miraculous new birth occurs within the believer by which one comes into possession of the very life of God.

The other is that the believer knows that he or she has this life.[11]

There is no mistaking that Hodges sees regeneration as a consequence or result of faith. Regeneration occurs because of faith. For Hodges faith clearly precedes regeneration, which not only distances him from the I of TULIP but also from the T. Since he has the unregenerate person responding in faith to the gospel, he cannot possibly affirm the doctrine of moral inability that is essential to the Reformed view of radical corruption or total depravity. For this reason Hodges and others who define themselves as Dispensationalists are said by Gerstner to embrace a "spurious" form of Calvinism.

When speaking of the order of salvation (*ordo salutis*), Reformed theology always and everywhere insists that regeneration precedes faith. Regeneration precedes faith because it is a necessary condition for faith. Indeed, it is the *sine qua non* of faith. It is important to understand, however, that the *order* of salvation refers to a *logical* order, not necessarily a *temporal* order. For example, when we say that justification is by faith, we do not mean that faith occurs first, and then we are justified at some later time. We believe that at the very moment faith is present, justification occurs. There is no time lapse between faith and justification. They occur simultaneously. Why then do we say that faith *precedes* justification? Faith precedes justification in a logical sense, not a temporal sense. Justification is logically dependent on faith, not faith on justification. We do not have faith because we are justified; we are justified because we have faith.

Similarly when Reformed theology says regeneration precedes faith, it is speaking in terms of logical priority, not temporal priority. We cannot exercise saving faith until we have been regenerated, so we say faith is dependent on regeneration, not regeneration on faith. Hodges and all semi-Pelagians argue that regeneration is a result of faith and dependent on it. This assumes that the not-yet-regenerate person can exercise saving faith.

Again we are forced back to the question of the extent of original sin. If original sin involves moral inability, as Augustine and the magisterial Reformers insisted, then faith can occur only as the result of regeneration, and regeneration can occur only as a result of effectual or irresistible grace.

To say that the grace of regeneration is irresistible is simply to say that this grace, which is so vital to our salvation, is sovereign. This grace is dispensed sovereignly and freely by God. It is truly grace, with no mixture of human merit of any kind. By this grace the captives are set free and the dead in sin are raised to a new life. This is the manifest work of the tender mercy of God, who stoops to rescue his children from sin and death and who, as he did in the initial work of creation, takes pieces of clay that are spiritually lifeless and breathes into them the breath that quickens them.

Regeneration is a supernatural work, a monergistic work, a work that effects what God intends. It is the supernatural work of re-creation by which the dead are raised and brought to a state of *fides viva*, a living faith, through which they are saved and adopted into the family of God.

10

God's Preservation of the Saints

The P of TULIP stands for perseverance, the doctrine of the perseverance of the saints. Like other terms represented by the acrostic TULIP, *perseverance* is somewhat misleading. It suggests that the continuity of faith and obedience is accomplished by the believer alone. Indeed the believer does persevere in faith and godliness, but this is due to the gracious work of God in his behalf. More accurate than *perseverance* is *preservation*. We persevere because we are preserved by God. If left to our own strength, none of us would persevere. Only because we are preserved by grace are we able to persevere at all.

A simple way to remember the essence of the doctrine of perseverance is to learn this ditty: "If we have it, we never lose it. If we lose it, we never had it." This is a "cute" way of affirming that full and final apostasy is never the lot of the Christian. Another shorthand expression of this doctrine is the aphorism "Once saved, always saved." This is sometimes called eternal security, since it calls attention to the enduring power of the salvation wrought for us and in us by the work of Christ.

Table 10.1
The TULIP's Fifth Petal

1	**T**otal depravity	Humanity's radical corruption
2	**U**nconditional election	God's sovereign choice
3	**L**imited atonement	Christ's purposeful atonement
4	**I**rresistible grace	The Spirit's effective call
5	**Perseverance of the saints**	God's preservation of the saints

The doctrine of perseverance has to do with the permanency of our salvation. The verb *to save* appears in the Bible in various tenses. We have been saved, are being saved, and shall be saved. There is a past, present, and future dimension to salvation. Our salvation began in eternity, is realized in time, and looks forward to heaven. The New Testament speaks of enduring to the end, promising that "he who endures to the end shall be saved" (Matt. 24:13). This may be understood as a condition or proviso for salvation or as a veiled promise of eternal salvation. Endurance in faith is a condition for future salvation. Only those who endure in faith will be saved for eternity.

This raises the obvious question, Are there some who have genuine faith who do not endure to the end and are therefore not ultimately saved? The semi-Pelagian answers yes. Semi-Pelagianism teaches that a person may come to true, authentic, saving faith and fall away from that faith, losing his salvation. This is clearly what the Roman

Catholic church teaches. Rome's system of sacramental theology provides for penance, the restoration to salvation of those who have fallen away. Penance is called the "second plank of salvation for those who have made shipwreck of their faith."

Rome prescribes penance for those who have committed mortal sin after having received the grace of justification. This sin is called "mortal" because it kills the grace of justification. Rome distinguishes between mortal and venial sins. Venial sin is real sin but not so serious as to destroy the grace of justification. By contrast, mortal sin is so serious, so egregious, that it causes a person to lose his salvation. He may regain his salvation and be restored to a state of justification by the sacrament of penance. For Rome as for all forms of semi-Pelagianism, no one can have positive assurance of perseverance except for a few saints who receive a special divine revelation to that effect.

The doctrine of the assurance of salvation differs from the doctrine of the perseverance of the saints, but it is closely related. The two doctrines may be distinguished from one another, but they can never be separated. Reformed theology affirms both the assurance of salvation and the perseverance of the saints.

Assurance of Salvation

The Westminster Confession of Faith declares:

> Although hypocrites and other unregenerate men may vainly deceive themselves with false hopes and carnal presumptions of being in the favour of God, and estate of

231

salvation (which hope of theirs shall perish): yet such as truly believe in the Lord Jesus, and love Him in sincerity, endeavouring to walk in all good conscience before Him, may, in this life, be certainly assured that they are in the state of grace, and may rejoice in the hope of the glory of God, which hope shall never make them ashamed.[1]

The confession acknowledges that there is such a thing as false assurance. False assurance is derived from an incorrect view of salvation or an incorrect assumption about one's personal faith. The possibility of false assurance does not eliminate the possibility of true or genuine assurance. The apostle Peter exhorts believers to seek the true assurance promised in the gospel: "Therefore, brethren, be even more diligent to make your calling and election sure, for if you do these things you will never stumble; for so an entrance will be supplied to you abundantly into the everlasting kingdom of our Lord and Savior Jesus Christ. Therefore I will not be negligent to remind you always of these things, though you know them, and are established in the present truth" (2 Pet. 1:10–12).

The apostle calls us to pursue assurance with diligence. It is the assurance of our election, which translates into an assurance of our salvation. All the elect are saved, so if we can be sure that we are the elect, we can also be sure that we are saved. To what end does the apostle exhort us to make our election sure? "If you do these things," he says, "you will never stumble."

What does this mean? Does it mean that if we gain an assurance of our election, we will never trip up and sin? Obviously not. The Bible is replete with examples of elect and saved people who fall into sin. Assurance does not guarantee perfection. So in what sense is it true that assurance means we will never stumble? This question is not easy to answer. Is the stumbling to which Peter refers so serious that we actually fall out of a state of salvation? Perhaps. Or is the apostle stressing the role of assurance in the believer's steady, sure-footed growth toward sanctification? Perhaps this is what Peter means, and his use of the term *never* is a case of apostolic hyperbole. I do not know for sure.

One thing, however, is certain. There is clearly a link between our assurance and our sanctification. The person who lacks assurance of salvation is vulnerable to a myriad of threats to his personal growth. The confident Christian, certain of his salvation, is free from the paralyzing fear that can inhibit personal growth. Without assurance we are assailed by doubt and uncertainty with respect to God's promises, which serve as an anchor for our souls.

It is of utmost importance that new Christians become certain of their personal salvation. Such assurance is a mighty boon to the growth of faith to maturity. The *Westminster Confession* continues:

This certainty is not a bare conjectural and probable persuasion grounded upon a fallible hope; but an infallible assurance of faith founded upon the divine truth of the promises of salvation, the inward evidence of those graces unto which these promises are made, the testimony of the Spirit of adoption witnessing with our spirits that we are the children of God, which Spirit is the earnest of our inheritance, whereby we are sealed to the day of redemption.[2]

This section of the confession is filled with crucial theological content. First we see the contrast between conjecture and certainty. The certainty of our assurance rests on an infallible basis. This basis is not *our* infallibility, but that of the One who grants it. It is based on a truth that is divine, a truth that comes from God himself. It rests on the "promises of salvation." We know that all human beings are covenant breakers, breaking promises, violating oaths, and failing to fulfill vows. We are all capable and guilty of such trespasses against the sanctity of truth. But unlike fallen humanity, God is absolutely a covenant keeper. He is incapable of lying, and he never breaks vows, oaths, or promises. He is the supreme Promise Keeper. His promises are clearly recorded for us in sacred Scripture, and these promises are corroborated and confirmed inwardly by the sure and certain testimony of the Holy Spirit himself, who is not only holy, but also the veritable Spirit of Truth.

The confession alludes to two New Testament affirmations regarding the Holy Spirit's work in our lives: he is the *earnest* of our inheritance and he *seals* us to the day of redemption. The term *earnest* came from the language of commerce. We use the term *earnest* to refer to actions motivated by a sincere and passionate zeal. We also use it occasionally in the field of modern commerce, particularly with reference to the buying of homes or other property. When signing a real estate contract, the buyer often puts down a deposit called "pin money" or "earnest money." It is called earnest money because it demonstrates that the buyer is entering into the contract "in earnest" and fully intends to pay all of the money owed.

Sometimes people who put up earnest money renege on the deal and fail to pay the full amount. Their failure belies the genuine earnestness of the down payment. But the Holy Spirit of Truth could never renege on a promise. When God gives us the earnest of the Spirit, he promises to finish what he has begun. His promise to complete the arrangement in the future cannot fail to come to pass. When God gives an earnest, nothing can vitiate his divine guarantee.

In addition to receiving "the earnest of our inheritance," we are "sealed" by the Spirit. The idea of sealing is drawn from the ancient practice of sealing special royal documents. Documents were authenticated by pressing the king's signet ring into wax, leaving an indelible impression that indicates royal ownership and authorization. In a sense the Spirit acts as the signet ring of the divine King. He makes an indelible mark on our souls, indicating his ownership of us. A seal was also used to prevent an invasion. Just as the tomb of Christ was sealed to prevent desecration by thieves and robbers, so we are sealed to prevent the evil one from snatching us from the arms of Christ.

Together the promises of God, the internal testimony of the Holy Spirit, the earnest of the Spirit, and the sealing of the Spirit comprise a solid ground for the believer's full assurance of salvation.

Assurance and Sanctification

The *Westminster Confession* adds:

> This infallible assurance doth not so belong to the essence of faith, but that a true believer may wait long, and conflict with many difficulties, before he be[comes a] partaker

of it: yet, being enabled by the Spirit to know the things which are freely given him of God, he may, without extraordinary revelation, in the right use of ordinary means, attain thereunto. And therefore it is the duty of every one to give all diligence to make his calling and election sure, that thereby his heart may be enlarged in peace and joy in the Holy Ghost, in love and thankfulness to God, and in strength and cheerfulness in the duties of obedience, the proper fruits of this assurance; so far is it from inclining men to looseness.[3]

The Westminster Assembly of Divines make it clear that assurance of salvation is not a necessary condition of salvation. We do not have to know that we are saved in order to be saved. This is what the confession means when it says that assurance does not "belong to the essence of faith." Assurance is a fruit of faith and may, indeed ultimately should, accompany faith. But assurance is not an essential of saving faith, in that we may be saved without it. For example, personal trust in Christ is an essential of saving faith. Any faith that lacks such trust is not saving faith because it lacks an essential element.

Though assurance is not essential to faith, it is nevertheless extremely important. The ancient distinction between the being or *esse* of a matter or thing, and the *well-being* or *bene esse* of a matter or thing, may be helpful. Assurance of salvation is not of the essence or being (*esse*) of the Christian life, but it is of the well-being (*bene esse*) of the Christian life. Assurance of salvation is important because it is linked to our growth in sanctification.

Full assurance is not an automatic fruit of conversion, nor is it necessarily an immediate fruit. The believer may be in a state of saving grace for a long time before attaining assurance. But attaining it is not a remote possibility; it is eminently attainable and surely desirable. The assurance of salvation is an enormous benefit to the Christian, yet it is also to be pursued as a duty. The confession alludes to the apostolic injunction to make our election and calling sure.

The believer is to pursue assurance so that "his heart may be enlarged in peace and joy in the Holy Ghost, in love and thankfulness to God, and in strength and cheerfulness in the duties of obedience." Assurance is connected with the fruit of the Holy Spirit, and this fruit is the very essence of our sanctification. Assurance then does not promote a false ease in Zion, or a smug or complacent form of spirituality, or (God forbid) a license for loose living. It promotes such things as love and thankfulness to God. These two elements, love and thankfulness, are the motivation for Christian obedience. My professor in graduate school, G. C. Berkouwer, once remarked in class, "The essence of theology is grace; the essence of ethics is gratitude." Berkouwer was getting at the inseparable relationship between the Christian's obedience and his gratefulness for having been saved by grace.

The confession concludes by declaring:

> True believers may have the assurance of their salvation divers ways shaken, diminished, and intermitted; as, by negligence in preserving of it, by falling into some special sin which woundeth the conscience and grieveth the Spirit; by some sudden or vehement temptation, by God's withdrawing the light of His countenance, and suffering even such as fear Him to walk in darkness and to have no light: yet are they never utterly destitute of that seed of God,

and life of faith, that love of Christ and the brethren, that sincerity of heart, and conscience of duty, out of which, by the operation of the Spirit, this assurance may, in due time, be revived; and by the which, in the mean time, they are supported from utter despair.[4]

This section reveals clearly that the Westminster Assembly of Divines did not divorce theology from the Christian life. They show keen insight into the manifold temptations that assail the ordinary Christian. They recognize that assurance is not frozen in concrete, incapable of augmentation or diminution. Our faith and assurance tend to be frail and fragile. Assurance can be easily disrupted and rudely shaken. It can be intermittent. It is particularly vulnerable to sin.

What Christian has not undergone what Martin Luther called the *Anfectung*, the "unbridled assault" of Satan? We are faced daily with manifold temptations, some of them grievous in nature and intensity, and we all too often succumb to them. Sin is the great enemy of assurance. When we commit it, we ask ourselves, "How can a true Christian do such things?" Then we must flee to Christ in confession and repentance, seeking his pardon and finding our solace in the Consolation of Israel. He alone can restore us to the joy of our salvation and the assurance of it.

When our consciences are seriously wounded, we may enter into what saints of the past have called "the dark night of the soul." This state is indescribably horrible for the believer, accompanied not by a glorious sense of God's presence but by a dreadful sense of his absence. We can feel totally abandoned by God, and in our spirit we may approach the rim of the abyss of hell. We experience what is declared by the apostle Paul:

> But we have this treasure in earthen vessels, that the excellence of the power may be of God and not of us. We are hard pressed on every side, yet not crushed; we are perplexed, but not in despair; persecuted, but not forsaken; struck down, but not destroyed—always carrying about in the body the dying of the Lord Jesus, that the life of Jesus also may be manifested in our body. For we who live are always delivered to death for Jesus' sake, that the life of Jesus also may be manifested in our mortal flesh. So then death is working in us, but life in you. But since we have the same spirit of faith, according to what is written, "I believed and therefore I spoke," we also believe and therefore speak, knowing that He who raised up the Lord Jesus will also raise us up with Jesus, and will present us with you. For all things are for your sakes, that grace, having spread through the many, may cause thanksgiving to abound to the glory of God.
>
> Therefore we do not lose heart. Even though our outward man is perishing, yet the inward man is being renewed day by day. (2 Cor. 4:7–16)

Paul speaks of being hard pressed, but not crushed; perplexed, but not in despair. When enduring the dark night of the soul, we come very close to despair. What assurance of salvation we have we cling to by our fingernails. Despair crowds in on us but does not finally absorb us. Though the light of God's countenance may be severely dimmed, it is never altogether extinguished. The Spirit always preserves for our troubled soul a ray of hope, no matter how dim it appears at the moment. The Christian may feel faint in heart, but he does not lose heart completely. Though the outward man is perishing, the inward man is being renewed day by day.

The anchor of the saint is his experience of God's tender mercy every morning. Though our assurance may stumble and crash for a season, the Holy Spirit revives it again and again. Even when we grieve the Holy Spirit and are chastised by the Father, the Spirit is not vindictive. He expresses grief over our sin, but he does not destroy us or abandon us to hell. The Father corrects those whom he loves and brings them to the fullness of salvation.

The Puritans were deeply concerned about assurance and its relationship to the Christian life. They echoed the view of *The Westminster Confession of Faith*. They refused to make justification depend on assurance, but they insisted on an organic relationship between justifying faith and assurance. Joel R. Beeke, in his marvelous work *Assurance of Faith*, writes:

> This distinction between faith and assurance had profound doctrinal and pastoral implications for the Puritans. To make justification dependent upon assurance would compel the believer to rely upon his own subjective condition rather than on the sufficiency of a triune God in the order of redemption. Such reliance is not only unsound doctrine, but also bears adverse pastoral affects. God does not require full and perfect faith, but sincere and "unfeigned" faith. Fulfillment of God's promises depends on the matter received, Christ's righteousness, and not upon the degree of assurance exercised in the receiving. If salvation depended on the full assurance of faith, John Downame observes, many would despair for then "the

palsied hand of faith should not receive Christ." Happily, salvation's sureness does not rest on the believer's sureness of his salvation, for "believers do not have the same assurance of grace and favor of God, nor do the same ones have it at all times." Pastorally, it is critical to maintain that justifying faith and the experience of doubt often coexist.[5]

Perseverance in Salvation

We have seen the close link between the assurance of salvation and perseverance in the Christian life. We must also remember, however, that they are not to be identified with or equated to each other. They are to be distinguished, but not separated. Assurance is our subjective confidence in both our present salvation and, by extension, our future salvation.

Some believe that a believer can have assurance about his present state of redemption but no certainty of his future state. He may be confident that at the moment he is in a state of grace, but he may lack assurance that he will continue in that state. They believe it is possible to fall away from grace and to lose the salvation one presently enjoys.

The Reformed faith believes that we can have assurance not only of our present state of salvation, but also of our continuity in that state. This assurance for the future rests in the doctrine of the perseverance of the saints.

The *Westminster Confession* declares:

They, whom God hath accepted in His Beloved, effectually called, and sanctified by His Spirit, can neither totally nor finally fall away from the state of grace, but shall certainly persevere therein to the end, and be eternally saved.[6]

We are accepted in God's "Beloved," a reference of course to Christ. The grounds of our justification are the merit of grace, merit of no mere temporary value but of eternal value and efficacy. The merit of grace perseveres in our behalf. Our election is likewise in Christ, and there is absolutely no danger or possibility that he will lose his own election. The question is, Will he lose those whom God has elected in him and with him?

The confession says that the elect (those whom God has accepted in Christ) cannot totally or finally fall away from the state of grace. The term *can* refers to ability, so this assertion means it is impossible for the elect to fully or finally fall from grace. It is possible, however, for the believer to experience a serious and radical fall. Scripture is replete with examples of believers who fell into grievous sin, such as David and Peter. Though their fall was dreadful, it was neither full nor final. Both were restored to repentance and grace. Believers can have a radical fall, but such falls are temporary and impermanent.

We have all known people who have made professions of faith and exhibited zeal for Christ, only to repudiate their confessions and turn away from Christ. What should we make of this? We consider two possibilities.

The first possibility is that their profession was not genuine in the first place. They confessed Christ with their mouths and then later committed a real apostasy from that confession. They are like the seed that fell in shallow soil and sprang up quickly, then withered and died (Matt. 13:5–6). The seed never really took root. They gave some outward signs of conversion, but their conversion was not genuine. They are like those who honored Christ with their lips but whose hearts were far from him (Matt. 15:7–8). Their faith was spurious from the beginning.

Into this category we can readily assign Judas (Jesus declared that he was of the devil from the beginning) and those about whom John says this:

> They went out from us, but they were not of us; for if they had been of us, they would have continued with us; but they went out that they might be made manifest, that none of them were of us. But you have an anointing from the Holy One, and you know all things. I have not written to you because you do not know the truth, but because you know it, and that no lie is of the truth. Who is a liar but he who denies that Jesus is the Christ? He is antichrist who denies the Father and the Son. Whoever denies the Son does not have the Father either; he who acknowledges the Son has the Father also.
>
> Therefore let that abide in you which you heard from the beginning. If what you heard from the beginning abides in you, you also will abide in the Son and in the Father. And this is the promise that He has promised us—eternal life. (1 John 2:19–25)

John acknowledges that some did leave the company of believers. They were apostates. But John declares that they were really not "of us." Their departure manifested their true state. Those who departed are contrasted with those who are anointed by God, those who have his Word abiding in them. If that Word truly abides in them, then they will abide in Christ and receive the promise of eternal life.

The second possible explanation of those who make a profession of faith, give outward evidence of conversion, and then repudiate the faith, is that they are true believers who have fallen into serious and radical apostasy but who will repent of their sin and be restored before they die. If they persist in apostasy until death, then theirs is a full and final fall from grace, which is evidence that they were not genuine believers in the first place.

The semi-Pelagian position offers a third possibility: such persons were truly converted, had true faith and salvation, and then fell away from faith and were fully and finally lost. This view denies the doctrine of the perseverance of the saints. It allows for the full and final loss of salvation on the part of those who once had genuinely received it.

Perseverance and Preservation

The *Westminster Confession* goes on to say:

> This perseverance of the saints depends not upon their own free will, but upon the immutability of the decree of election, flowing from the free and unchangeable love of God the Father; upon the efficacy of the merit and intercession of Jesus Christ, the abiding of the Spirit, and of the seed of God within them, and the nature of the covenant of grace: from all which ariseth also the certainty and infallibility thereof.[7]

The perseverance of the saints could more accurately be called the preservation of the saints, as this affirmation of the Westminster Assembly of Divines makes clear. The believer does not persevere through the power of his un-aided will. God's preserving grace makes our perseverance both possible and actual. Even the regenerated person with a liberated will is still vulnerable to sin and temptation, and the residual power of sin is so strong that without the aid of grace the believer would, in all probability, fall away. But God's decree is immutable. His sovereign purpose to save his elect from the foundation of the world is not frustrated by our weakness.

Were the Bible to say nothing about perseverance, what it says about God's electing grace would be sufficient to convince us of the doctrine of perseverance. But the Bible is not silent on these matters, declaring clearly and often that God will finish what he has begun for us and in us. For example, Paul declares: "I thank my God upon every remembrance of you, always in every prayer of mine making request for you all with joy, for your fellowship in the gospel from the first day until now, being confident of this very thing, that He who has begun a good work in you will complete it until the day of Jesus Christ . . ." (Phil. 1:3–6).

Note that Paul puts the stress on God, not on man, when he says that "He who has begun a good work in you will complete it." What God begins he finishes. His work is not left dangling like some sublime, unfinished symphony. Christ is called both the Author and the Finisher of our redemption. We are his handiwork. As an expert Craftsman, he never needs to destroy or discard an imperfect work of spiritual artisanship.

God's preservation of the saints is not based on a mere, abstract deduction from his decree of election. It rests also on his immutable and free love, a love that is abiding, a love of complacency that nothing can sever. Again the apostle Paul declares:

> What then shall we say to these things? If God is for us, who can be against us? He who did not spare His own Son, but delivered Him up for us all, how shall He not with Him also freely give us all things? Who shall bring a charge against God's elect? It is God who justifies. Who is he who condemns? It is Christ who died, and furthermore is also risen, who is even at the right hand of God, who also makes intercession for us. Who shall separate us from the love of Christ? Shall tribulation, or distress, or persecution, or famine, or nakedness, or peril, or sword? As it is written: "For Your sake we are killed all day long; we are accounted as sheep for the slaughter." Yet in all these things we are more than conquerors through Him who loved us. For I am persuaded that neither death nor life, nor angels nor principalities nor powers, nor things present nor things to come, nor height nor depth, nor any other created thing, shall be able to separate us from the love of God which is in Christ Jesus our Lord. (Rom. 8:31–36)

Paul's list of things that conceivably could threaten or jeopardize Christ's love for his sheep is representative, not exhaustive. Paul is amplifying the general statement he made earlier, that *nothing* can separate us from the love of God that is ours in Christ Jesus. This love is enduring and permanent. We persevere in grace because God perseveres in his love toward us.

Neither is there any limit to the merit of the grace bestowed on us, or to Christ's perpetual intercession for us. Perhaps the strongest force enabling us to persevere is our High Priest's work of intercession in our behalf. Also contributing to our preservation are the Holy Spirit's abiding within us as our earnest and seal, the seed of God planted in our souls, and finally the very nature of the covenant of grace, by which God's promises to us are assured absolutely.

These assurances of perseverance are rooted in the idea expressed in the Latin phrase *Deus pro nobis,* "God for us." The apostle asks the rhetorical question "If God is for us, who can be against us?" Of course many are against us. We expect to be hated, and hated all the day long, because our Lord indicated this would be the case. We are despised by Satan and his minions. All of them stand in opposition to us. All who are of Antichrist (*anti* meaning either "against" or "in place of") are also anti-Christian.

When Paul asks, "Who shall be against us?" he means that no one (and nothing) will *prevail* against us. God's preservation results in our becoming "more than conquerors." This three-word phrase translates one Greek word, *hypernikon,* which is rendered in Latin by the word *supervincemus.* The prefixes *hyper* and *super* elevate the idea of conqueror to the highest level.

Just as the *Westminster Confession* indicates the possibility of the believer's temporary loss of assurance, so the confession recognizes that perseverance is not always a steady, upward progress of sanctification without serious lapses. True Christians may fall seriously and radically, but they cannot finally fall from grace. The confession declares:

> Nevertheless, they may, through the temptations of Satan and of the world, the prevalency of corruption remaining in them, and the neglect of the means of their preservation,

fall into grievous sins; and, for a time, continue therein: whereby they incur God's displeasure, and grieve His Holy Spirit, come to be deprived of some measure of their graces and comforts, have their hearts hardened, and their consciences wounded; hurt and scandalize others, and bring temporal judgments upon themselves.[8]

As part of the process of our sanctification, perseverance is a synergistic work. This means it is a cooperative effort between God and us. We persevere as he preserves. An analogy of this is often used with children. A child and his father walk down a dangerous path while holding hands. There are two ways in which they can hold hands. First, the child can grasp his father's hand and hold on tightly. If he lets go, he may fall. Second, the father can hold the child's hand. Only if the father loosens his grip can the child fall. In the first instance the child's safety depends on the consistency and firmness by which he clings to his father. In the second instance the child's safety depends on the consistency and firmness by which the father clings to him.

We may push the analogy a bit and say that when the child loosens his grip on the father's hand, the father may let him stumble and scrape his knees. Though the child incurs the father's displeasure in the process, the father will not allow his grip on the child to be loosed entirely, preventing him from falling into an abyss.

Even though God is holding on to us, we are to hold on to him at the same time. We are capable of losing our grip, and indeed we do so. We have a responsibility to hold on as tightly as we can, even though we are sure he will not let us go. The New Testament frequently admonishes us to do this and warns us of the consequences of letting go. We can fall from grace, but not absolutely. At times Scripture seems to forbid what is ultimately impossible and to command what is also impossible. For example, it calls us to be perfect as our heavenly Father is perfect (Matt. 5:48). No one can reach this degree of perfection. Why then does Scripture speak in this manner? Luther called this the "evangelical usage of the law." He meant that the gospel calls us to strive as diligently as we can to meet the highest standards of the law. Such calls drive us to an ever increasing dependence on grace.

The Problem of Hebrews

Perhaps the most disputed biblical text regarding the perseverance of the saints is one found in the book of Hebrews: "For it is impossible for those who were once enlightened, and have tasted the heavenly gift, and have become partakers of the Holy Spirit, and have tasted the good word of God and the powers of the age to come, if they fall away, to renew them again to repentance, since they crucify again for themselves the Son of God, and put Him to an open shame" (6:4–6).

The apostle warns that certain people cannot be restored to salvation if they do certain things. The first question is, What kind of people is he describing? Are they Christians or non-Christians? At first glance the answer appears to be obvious. These people have been enlightened, have tasted the heavenly gift, and have partaken of the Holy Spirit, so they must be believers.

At least one other possibility, however, needs to be explored. The Old Testament is clear that not all who were *in*

Israel were *of* Israel. Some who were in the covenant community did not possess genuine faith. And Christ said that in his church tares would grow among the wheat (Matt. 13:24–25). For this reason there has always been a distinction between those who belong to the visible church and those who are part of the invisible church. As Augustine suggested, the invisible church, the body of elect believers, exists substantially within the visible church. It is called "invisible" because God alone can read the true condition of the human heart. The soul is invisible to us.

All that is said in Hebrews 6 could be said of unbelieving members of the visible church with one possible exception. In a sense all members of the visible church are enlightened and taste the heavenly gift. But can unbelieving members be said to have repented? The phrase "renew them again to repentance" presupposes that they have repented at least once in the past. If repentance is, as Reformed theology believes, a fruit of regeneration, then the author of Hebrews is describing people who have been regenerated. Might their repentance have been false or spurious like Esau's? Spurious repentance can hardly be in view because there would be no value in the renewal of such repentance. This reference to repentance convinces me that the author is describing regenerate Christians.

This conclusion leaves me with only two options: (1) either regenerate Christians can fall away permanently and we must abandon the doctrine of the perseverance of the saints or (2) the admonition in Hebrews 6 is an example of what Luther called an "evangelical usage of the law."

The issue here must be settled by allowing Scripture to interpret Scripture, not by setting one portion of Scripture against another. If the rest of Scripture is clear regarding perseverance (and I believe it is), then we must interpret what is ambiguous here by what is unambiguous elsewhere. The implicit must always be interpreted by the explicit, the unclear by the clear. The author of Hebrews nowhere states that a true believer does in fact do what he is warning believers not to do.

If no believer does what the author warns against, why bother with such a warning? We must be exceedingly careful here. Is this really a warning, or is it more properly speaking an argument? Frequently in the New Testament we see examples of what is called *ad hominem* argument, an argument that is "to the man." There are two types of *ad hominem* argument, one that is invalid and one that is valid. The so-called *ad hominem abusive* argument attacks the person rather than his argument. The valid *ad hominem* argument, called *reductio ad absurdum*, adopts the other person's premises and takes them to their logical conclusion, which is an absurdity. Paul uses this type of argument, for example, in 1 Corinthians. It follows an if-then pattern of reasoning: "If Christ is not risen, [then] your faith is futile" (15:17).

It would be helpful if we knew who wrote Hebrews, to whom he was writing, and most importantly the occasion for his writing them. We do not know for sure the exact issue or exactly what threatened the Hebrew Christians. If the issue was the Judaizer heresy that posed a major threat to the early church, then such an *ad hominem* argument would make sense. The Judaizer heresy required that believers return to the obligations of the Old Covenant law, which would place them again under the curse that had been lifted by Christ. This would be a tacit repudiation of Christ's atonement, requiring a fresh atonement, a recrucifixion. But a recrucifixion is impossible. If one did in fact return to the old status, there would be no provision left for this person's salvation.

I believe the author is arguing in this way and is not declaring that true believers do in fact commit this sin. The author's later statement lends support to this interpretation:

> But, beloved, we are confident of better things concerning you, yes, things that accompany salvation, though we speak in this manner. For God is not unjust to forget your work and labor of love which you have shown toward His name, in that you have ministered to the saints, and do minister. And we desire that each one of you show the same diligence to the full assurance of hope until the end, that you do not become sluggish, but imitate those who through faith and patience inherit the promises. (Heb. 6:9–12)

Note that the author says, "But . . ." *But* introduces a weighty qualifier: "we are confident of better things concerning you, yes, things that accompany salvation, though we speak in this manner." The reference to speaking in a particular manner should alert us to the danger of drawing rash and unwarranted conclusions. This entire admonition is given in a "manner of speaking." The author expresses confidence that the people he addresses will not do the things he has warned against but that they will do that which accompanies salvation. This confidence lies at the heart of the doctrine of the perseverance of the saints. The God who has begun a good work in us will complete that work to the end, both fully and finally, as the golden chain of redemption reaches its ultimate, ordained end.

Notes

Introduction: Reformed Theology *Is* a Theology

1. Adolf Harnack, *What Is Christianity?*, trans. Thomas Bailey Saunders (1901; reprint, New York: Harper & Row, 1957).

2. David F. Wells, *No Place for Truth: or, Whatever Happened to Evangelical Theology?* (Grand Rapids, Mich.: Eerdmans, 1993), 95.

3. Ibid., 97. See Ian T. Ramsey, *Models for Divine Activity* (London: SCM, 1973), 1.

4. Wells, *No Place for Truth*, 98.

Chapter 1 Centered on God

1. Martin Luther, *What Luther Says: An Anthology*, ed. Ewald M. Plass, 3 vols. (St. Louis: Concordia, 1959), 2:551.

2. John Calvin, *Institutes of the Christian Religion*, 2 vols., trans. Henry Beveridge (1845; reprint, Grand Rapids, Mich.: Eerdmans, 1964), 1:51 (1.5.1).

3. Ibid.

4. Ibid., 1:37 (1.1.1).

5. Ibid., 1:38–39 (1.1.2).

6. *The Westminster Confession of Faith*, 2.2.

7. Calvin, *Institutes of the Christian Religion*, 1:39 (1.1.3).

8. Ibid., 1:59–60 (1.5.11–12).

Chapter 2 Based on God's Word Alone

1. John Calvin, *Institutes of the Christian Religion*, 2 vols., trans. Henry Beveridge (1845; reprint, Grand Rapids, Mich.: Eerdmans, 1964), 1:68 (1.7.1).

2. Martin Luther, *What Luther Says: An Anthology*, ed. Ewald M. Plass, 3 vols. (St. Louis: Concordia, 1959), 1:62.

3. Ibid., 1:63.

4. Ibid., 1:67.

5. Ibid., 1:68.

6. Ibid., 1:72.

7. Ibid., 1:87.

8. Ibid., 1:88.

9. Calvin, *Institutes of the Christian Religion*, 1:68–69 (1.7.1).

10. Ibid., 1:69 (1.7.2).

11. Luther, *What Luther Says*, 1:87.

12. Ibid.

13. Ibid., 1:93.

14. Ibid., 1:91–92.

Chapter 3 Committed to Faith Alone

1. Martin Luther, *What Luther Says: An Anthology*, ed. Ewald M. Plass, 3 vols. (St. Louis: Concordia, 1959), 2:704 n. 5.

2. Ibid., 2:704.

3. Ibid., 2:703.

4. John Calvin, *Institutes of the Christian Religion*, 2 vols., trans. Henry Beveridge (1845; reprint, Grand Rapids, Mich.: Eerdmans, 1964), 2:37–38 (3.11.2).

5. Luther, *What Luther Says*, 2:921.

6. Ibid., 2:710.

7. Calvin, *Institutes of the Christian Religion*, 2:115 (3.17.12).

8. Ibid., 2:57 (3.11.21).

9. Luther, *What Luther Says*, 1:522.

10. Ibid., 2:714–15.

Chapter 4 Devoted to the Prophet, Priest, and King

1. *The Westminster Confession of Faith*, 8.1.

Chapter 5 Nicknamed Covenant Theology

1. C. I. Scofield, ed., *Scofield Reference Bible* (New York: Oxford University, 1909).

2. George E. Mendenhall, *Law and Covenant in Israel and the Ancient Near East* (Pittsburgh: Biblical Colloquium, 1955).

3. Meredith G. Kline, *Treaty of the Great King: The Covenant Structure of Deuteronomy: Studies and Commentary* (Grand Rapids, Mich.: Eerdmans, 1963); *By Oath Consigned: A Reinterpretation of the Covenant Signs of Circumcision and Baptism* (Grand Rapids, Mich.: Eerdmans, 1968).

4. *The Westminster Confession of Faith*, 22.1–2.

5. Ibid., 7.2.

6. Ibid., 7.3. Emphasis added.

7. Ibid., 7.5–6.

Chapter 6 Humanity's Radical Corruption

1. Adolf Harnack, *History of Dogma*, trans. James Millar (1898; reprint, New York: Dover, 1961), 168–69. From Augustine, *On the Gift of Perseverance* (AD 428), 53.

2. John Calvin, *Institutes of the Christian Religion*, 2 vols., trans. Henry Beveridge (1845; reprint, Grand Rapids, Mich.: Eerdmans, 1964), 1:214 (2.1.5).

3. Martin Luther, *What Luther Says: An Anthology*, ed. Ewald M. Plass, 3 vols. (St. Louis: Concordia, 1959), 3:1300–1301.

4. *The Westminster Confession of Faith*, 9.3.

5. Calvin, *Institutes of the Christian Religion*, 1:228–29 (2.2.6–7).

6. *The Westminster Confession*, 9.4–5.

Chapter 7 God's Sovereign Choice

1. *The Westminster Confession of Faith*, 3.3–5. The word *predestined* is *predestinated* in the original.

2. Albrecht Oepke, "*Elkō*," in Gerhard Kittel, ed., *Theological Dictionary of the New Testament*, ed. and trans. Geoffrey W. Bromiley, vol. 2 (Grand Rapids, Mich.: Eerdmans, 1964), 503.

3. John Calvin, *A Treatise on the Eternal Predestination of God*, trans. Henry Cole, in *Calvin's Calvinism* (Grand Rapids, Mich.: Eerdmans, 1950), 31.

4. John Calvin, *Institutes of the Christian Religion*, 2 vols., trans. Henry Beveridge (1845; reprint, Grand Rapids, Mich.: Eerdmans, 1964), 2:212 (3.22.1).

Chapter 8 Christ's Purposeful Atonement

1. J. I. Packer, "Introductory Essay," in John Owen, *The Death of Death in the Death of Christ: A Treatise in Which the Whole Controversy about Universal Redemption Is Fully Discussed* (1852; reprint, London: Banner of Truth, 1959), 4.

2. Ibid.

3. Owen, *The Death of Death in the Death of Christ*, 161.

4. Ibid., 236.

5. *The Westminster Confession of Faith*, 3.1.

6. Ibid.

7. Owen, *The Death of Death in the Death of Christ*, 45.

Chapter 9 The Spirit's Effective Call

1. J. I. Packer and O. R. Johnston, "Historical and Theological Introduction," in Martin Luther, *The Bondage of the Will*, trans. J. I. Packer and O. R. Johnston (Cambridge: James Clarke / Westwood, N.J.: Revell, 1957), 57–58.

2. Ibid., p. 58. See Martin Luther, *Vom unfreien Willen*, ed. H. J. Iwand (1954), 253.

3. Luther, *The Bondage of the Will*, 78.

4. Packer and Johnston, "Historical and Theological Introduction," 58–59.

5. Ibid., 59.

6. *The Westminster Confession of Faith*, 10.1. The phrase has *predestined* is hath *predestinated* in the original.

7. John Calvin, *Institutes of the Christian Religion*, 2 vols., trans. Henry Beveridge (1845; reprint, Grand Rapids, Mich.: Eerdmans, 1964), 2:240 (3.24.1). From Augustine, *On the Predestination of the Saints*, trans. R. E. Wallis, in *Basic Writings of Saint Augustine*, ed. Whitney J. Oates, 2 vols. (1948; reprint, Grand Rapids, Mich.: Baker, 1992), 1:790 (chap. 13). Compare Wallis's translation of this passage: "This grace, therefore, which is hiddenly bestowed in human hearts by the Divine gift, is rejected by no hard heart, because it is given for the sake of first taking away the hardness of the heart. When, therefore, the Father is heard within, and teaches, so that a man comes to the Son, He takes away the heart of stone and gives a heart of flesh, as in the declaration of the prophet He has promised. Because He thus makes them children and vessels of mercy which He has prepared for glory."

8. John H. Gerstner, *Wrongly Dividing the Word of Truth: A Critique of Dispensationalism* (Brentwood, Tenn.: Wolgemuth & Hyatt, 1991).

9. Zane C. Hodges, *Absolutely Free! A Biblical Reply to Lordship Salvation* (Dallas: Redención Viva / Grand Rapids, Mich.: Zondervan, 1989), 48.

10. Ibid., 49.

11. Ibid., 51–52.

Chapter 10 God's Preservation of the Saints

1. *The Westminster Confession of Faith*, 18.1.

2. Ibid., 18.2.

3. Ibid., 18.3.

4. Ibid., 18.4.

5. Joel R. Beeke, *Assurance of Faith: Calvin, English Puritanism, and the Dutch Second Reformation*, American University Studies: Theology and Religion, series 7, vol. 89 (New York: Lang, 1991), 143. The first quotation is from John Downame, *A Treatise of the True Nature and Definition of Justifying Faith* (1635), 12–13. The second quotation is from William Ames, *Medulla ss. theologiae . . . extracts & methodice disposita* (1627), 1.27.19.

6. *The Westminster Confession*, 17.1.

7. Ibid., 17.2.

8. Ibid., 17.3.

GLOSSARY
OF FOREIGN TERMS

The foreign words in this glossary are Latin unless otherwise specified (Germ. = German, Gk. = Greek).

abscondito (hidden)

accidens (external, perceivable qualities)

ad hominem (to the man)

agnus Dei (the lamb of God)

Anfectung Germ. (unbridled assault)

articulus stantis et cadentis ecclesiae (the article upon which the church stands falls)

aseity (existence originating from itself)

assensus (intellectual assent)

autographa Gk. (original manuscripts)

bene esse (well-being)

communicatio idiomata (communication of attributes)

con (with)

coram Deo (before the face of God)

de merito congrui et condigni (merit of congruence and worthiness)

de pactio (by pact or covenant)

Deus absconditus (hidden God)

Deus pro nobis (God for us)

Deus revelatus (revealed God)

elkō Gk. (to drag)

equos (equal)

errare humanum est (to err is human)

esse (being, essence)

ethelodoulos Gk. (voluntary slave)

ex cathedra (from the chair)

extra nos (outside of us)

fabricum idolarum (fabricator of idols)

fides viva (vital, living faith)

fiducia (cognitive, affective, volitional faith)

259

finitum non capax infinitum (the finite cannot grasp [or contain] the infinite)

fundamentum (foundation)

gnosis Gk. (knowledge)

homoi-ousios Gk. (of similar or like substance)

homo-ousios Gk. (same essence, substance, being)

hypernikon Gk. (more than conquerors)

iustificare (justify, declare righteous)

liberium arbitrium (free will)

libertas (liberty)

massa peccati (mass of sin)

meritum de condigno (condign merit)

meritum de congruo (congruous merit)

monogenems Gk. (only begotten, unique)

monophysis Gk. (one nature, substance)

munus triplex (threefold office)

non posse non peccare (the inability not to sin)

non posse peccare (the inability to sin)

notae. See *notitia*

notitia (knowledge)

ordo salutis (order of salvation)

posse non peccare (the ability not to sin)

posse peccare (the ability to sin)

quadriga (four-fold method of interpretation)

radix (root)

recepimus (we receive)

reductio ad absurdum (reduce to absurdity)

revelato (revealed)

sacra Scriptura sui interpres (Holy Scripture is its own interpreter)

semper reformanda (always reforming)

sensus literalis (literal [or intended] sense)

simul iustus et peccator (at the same time just and sinner)

sine qua non (without which, not; something essential)

sola fide (faith alone)

sola gratia (grace alone)

sola Scriptura (Scripture alone)

soli Christo (Christ alone)

supervincemus (more than conquerors)

tertium quid (something related to two things but distinct from them; something intermediate between two things)

theopneustos Gk. (God-breathed)

ubi (where)

usus loquendi (usage of speech)

verbum Dei (Word of God)

vere Deus (truly God)

vere homo (truly man)

via affirmatas (way of affirmation)

via eminentia (way of eminence)

via negationis (way of negation)

vox Dei (voice of God)

Wesen Germ. (being, essence)

Index of Subjects

INDEX OF PERSONS

Index of Scripture

Dr. R. C. Sproul is founder and chairman of Ligonier Ministries, an international Christian education ministry located near Orlando, Florida. He is also copastor of Saint Andrew's Chapel in Sanford, Florida, chancellor of Reformation Bible College, and executive editor of *Tabletalk* magazine.

Dr. Sproul's teaching can be heard daily on the radio program *Renewing Your Mind*, which is broadcast on hundreds of radio outlets in the United States and in more than forty countries worldwide. He has produced more than three hundred lecture series and has recorded more than eighty video series on subjects such as the history of philosophy, theology, Bible study, apologetics, and Christian living.

Dr. Sproul has contributed dozens of articles to national evangelical publications; has spoken at conferences, churches, and schools around the world; and has written more than ninety books, including *The Holiness of God*, *Faith Alone*, and *Everyone's a Theologian*. He is also general editor of the *Reformation Study Bible* and has had a distinguished academic teaching career at various colleges and seminaries.

Dr. Sproul holds degrees from Westminster College, Pittsburgh Theological Seminary, the Free University of Amsterdam, and Whitefield Theological Seminary. He lives with his wife, Vesta, in Sanford, Florida.

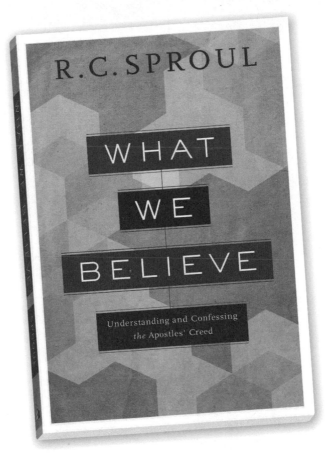

Also by
R. C. SPROUL

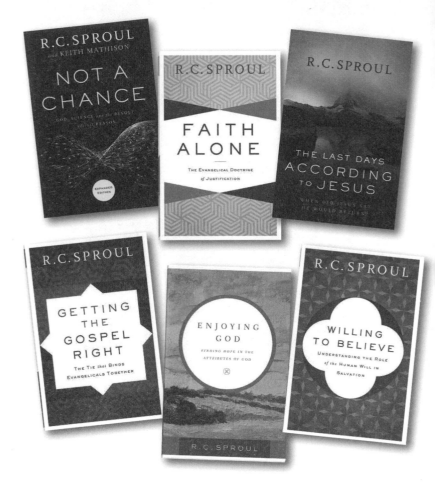